THE
ONSLAUGHT
THE GERMAN DRIVE TO STALINGRAD

THE
ONSLAUGHT
THE GERMAN DRIVE TO STALINGRAD

Documented in 150 unpublished
colour photographs from the
German Archive for Art and History

With an historical essay by
Heinrich, Graf von Einsiedel

Translated by Arnold J. Pomerans

Foreword by Max Hastings

W. W. NORTON & COMPANY
NEW YORK   LONDON

First published in the United States in 1985 by W.W. Norton & Company, Inc.
Originally published in West Germany in 1984 by Hoffmann and Campe Verlag, Hamburg,
under the title *Der Überfall*.

Text copyright © 1984 by Hoffman and Campe Verlag
This translation and foreword copyright © 1984 by Sidgwick and Jackson Limited, London
Illustrations copyright © 1984 by Archiv für Kunst und Geschichte, Berlin

ISBN 0-393-01939-X

Phototypeset by Falcon Graphic Art Ltd, Wallington, Surrey
Printed in Italy by New Interlitho SpA Milan
for W.W. Norton & Company, Inc.
500 Fifth Avenue, New York, New York 10110

CONTENTS

FOREWORD

For at least a generation after the Second World War, it was the natural conceit of the Western allies, and of their historians, to consider themselves the principal adversaries and vanquishers of Nazi Germany. It was the cherished belief of the British people that their stubborn resistance to Hitler in 1940 had inflicted a major setback upon his ambitions. Thereafter, in Western eyes, progress towards Hitler's eclipse hinged upon the bomber offensive and the long build-up of Allied strength that made possible the defeat of Germany's armies between 1943 and 1945 in North Africa, Italy, and finally North-West Europe.

Yet over the past twenty years, we have slowly been reassessing the evidence, and learning to look at the war in a global historical perspective. The fundamental reality is that the Eastern Front was the decisive theatre. The fighting power of the Red Army and the industrial might of the United States were the chief instruments of German defeat. From the earliest days of Nazism, Hitler's ambitions lay in the East. Although he was determined to tolerate no opposition to his will from France or Britain, he considered the two Western powers enemies of Germany only insofar as they threatened his other designs.

For Hitler reshaped the longstanding German yearning for *lebensraum* – living space. Where the Kaiser and his generation had focussed their demands upon colonies overseas, 'a place in the sun', Hitler was convinced that Germany must expand directly eastwards in pursuit of his vision of an Aryan superpower. He argued first, that if Germany merely stood on her existing borders, sooner or later the Aryans must be invaded and overrun by their vastly more numerous traditional enemies, the Slavonic races. Second, he believed that these nations of 'sub-humans', as he designated them, could provide both a massive labour force and a captive market for the economy of the Third Reich. When Russia had been conquered, he proposed that her people should become, in perpetuity, the uneducated slaves of the German Empire. These ambitions, perhaps more accurately obsessions, lay at the heart of German policy in the years before 1939, and the first months of war. The *anschluss* with Austria, the seizure of Czechoslovakia and the conquest of Poland were merely preliminaries to the great central task of Nazism. Hitler's relief at the signing of the Russo–German pact in August 1939 was prompted chiefly by his belief that it made Franco–British intervention in support of Poland seem impracticable and thus unlikely.

The Norwegian and French campaigns of 1940 were designed explicitly to remove the threat to Germany from the West before the great struggle in the East could begin. After the French surrender in June, Hitler confidently expected Britain to make peace, and was willing to offer terms that he considered generous to a power which he regarded as a natural racial ally. When Churchill declined to negotiate, Hitler allowed Goering to commence his air assault as an essential preliminary to possible invasion, but made it clear to his commanders that he was doubtful about mounting a land campaign. As he told Mussolini at a conference early that autumn, he now found himself in the position of a man with only one shot left in his rifle. If he invaded Britain, whatever the outcome he would be left without the resources for an early campaign in the East.

And Hitler was uncertain of an easy success in Britain. Beyond his essential respect for British powers of resistance, he knew that his own forces lacked specialized equipment for a major amphibious operation in the face of the Royal Navy. If Goering's Luftwaffe had indeed achieved a quick triumph over the RAF, it is possible that Hitler, the perpetual opportunist, would have proceeded with a seaborne assault. But with the air battle proving costly and inconclusive, Hitler determined to break off the action. He judged, correctly, that Britain possessed no armed force capable of interfering with German operations on the continent for years to come, if ever. By defeating France and neutralizing Britain, he had achieved his essential war aims in the West without needing to undertake further hazardous cross-Channel operations. He could safely turn his attention to his vast, fundamental designs in the East.

Ironically, while Stalin strove to maintain Nazi goodwill with shipments of oil and grain because of his profound terror that Russian national unity could not survive a war with Germany, Hitler constantly expected a

8

Russian attack. He had no trust in Stalin's good faith. The Red Army had been critically weakened by the loss of most of its competent officers in the Purges, and Stalin was suffering great difficulties in rebuilding and reinforcing his formations in the West. But Hitler told his own officers that the only dilemma for Germany was that of: 'Should we strike out first, or wait until we were overwhelmed some time in the future?' He held out to them the prospect that, with Russia's defeat, it should be simple to cajole or bludgeon France, Spain, Turkey and Iran into the war against Britain, which would then be compelled to accept the futility of further resistance. Some of his advisers and commanders remained sceptical about this scenario, and about the difficulty of conquering Russia. But their Führer's prestige and the aura of invincibility surrounding his judgements had never stood stronger. He had confounded his doubters on Poland, on Norway, and about the ease of victory in the West. No senior officer now offered serious resistance to his plan for Operation Barbarossa.

In the months preceding the invasion, while the Russians continued to reinforce his armies, Stalin utterly disbelieved reports from the British, based on their cipher-breaking intelligence, that a German onslaught was imminent. The Russian leader dismissed these as crude attempts to break the Russo–German Pact. Yet when Hitler received word of British overtures to Moscow, he seized upon the threat of an imminent Russo–British axis to justify German haste.

Yet, though he insisted that a single quick campaign would bring victory to the *Wehrmacht*, he was troubled by nagging fears. When Goering sought to flatter him with a vainglorious promise that the Führer's greatest triumph was at hand, Hitler sharply rebuked him: 'Goering, it will be our toughest struggle yet – by far the toughest. Why? Because for the first time we shall be fighting an *ideological* enemy, and an ideological enemy of fanatical persistence at that.' One day, at his new headquarters in East Prussia, specially constructed for Barbarossa, he voiced his concern about the Red Army's powers of resistance to his secretaries: 'We know absolutely nothing about Russia. It might be one big soap bubble, but it might just as well turn out to be very different.'

The German army attacked at 3 a.m. on the morning of 22 June 1941 with 140 divisions of which 17 were panzer and 13 mechanized; 7100 guns,

3300 tanks, 2770 aircraft . . . and 625,000 horses. Hitler sent forth his host, 3 million men in all, with a proclamation which concluded with the fervent words 'May the Lord God help us all in this struggle!' Within a week, the armies of Leeb, Bock, and von Rundstedt were deep inside Russia, sweeping all before them. Guderian's spearhead had advanced 270 miles. Hitler's staff asked why he had not troubled even to provide a pretext for invasion, far less issued a declaration of war. 'Nobody is ever asked about his motives at the bar of history,' he answered. 'Why did Alexander invade India? Why did the Romans fight their Punic wars, or Frederick II his second Silesian campaign? In history it is success alone that counts.'

A Russian commander was asked, after the war, at what moment he knew that the Red Army must emerge victorious. He replied: 'At 3 p.m. on 22 June.' His audience was mystified, for at that stage the Germans were smashing through everything in their path, capturing thousands of prisoners. The Russian sardonically amplified his statement: 'We could see that our men were fighting back.' Stalin's behaviour for months before the invasion had been dominated by grotesque terror that his own army would not fight, that, broken and demoralized by the Purges and the cruelties of his regime, his divisions would collapse absolutely. In reality, despite the huge initial setbacks, the chronic difficulties of resistance when a large part of the Russian air force was destroyed on the ground by the Luftwaffe and only a quarter of the Red tank force was serviceable, the Russian soldier was already demonstrating his extraordinary hardiness and courage.

Throughout the war, intelligence was one of the crippling weaknesses of Hitler's armies, never more so than in the launching of Barbarossa. The Germans critically underestimated the strength of the Russian army and the quality of its equipment, above all the T–34 tank. It is striking to observe that most German soldiers interviewed after 1945 revealed more respect for the material resources of the American and British armies than for the fighting power of their men. Yet almost all admitted a profound admiration for the Russian soldier. Whatever the poverty of his leadership, the clumsiness of his tactics, the shortcomings of his equipment and clothing, the Russian kept coming on, in a fashion unmatched among the armies of the Second World War.

It is a Western conceit to suppose that the struggle of 1939–45 was less bloody than that of 1914–18. In reality, Hitler's war was far more terrible and costly, but the bloodshed was concentrated in the East. It was in the East that the *Wehrmacht* was bled of 2 million dead between 1941 and 1944, before the first Allied soldier stepped ashore in Normandy. The Anglo–American campaigns in North Africa and Italy involved trifling forces, negligible casualties by comparison with the titanic conflict in Russia. While America lost less than 300,000 dead in the Second World War and Britain and France less than 500,000 each, Russia lost 20 million, Germany 5 million. As late as June 1944, while 59 German divisions awaited the Allies in the West, 156 divisions were committed in the East. On the Russian front, amid the appalling slaughter of civilians by the SS death squads, the ferocious Russian guerilla campaign met by hideous German reprisals, the greatest tank battles of history were fought out in conditions that, for many months of each year, defied human resistance.

As Hitler's hopes of a lightning victory in a single campaign in 1941 began to die, as reinforcements from Russia's eastern border began to stream west, the scale of the German miscalculation became apparent. Allied intelligence assessments of Germany's industrial potential were founded upon the misapprehension that in September 1939, the Reich had been fully mobilized for war. In reality, with extraordinary recklessness, Hitler had authorized only sufficient military production to support his immediate operational plans. After the victory in France in May 1940, he actually ordered reductions in some areas of munitions production. He was profoundly concerned to sustain German civilian morale and enthusiasm for the war by maintaining supplies of food and even luxury goods. In 1940, wholly unknown to the British, their own tank production was already outstripping that of the Reich. Britain was far more fully industrially mobilized than her principal enemy. Germany had never rearmed in depth. Reserves of every kind – tanks, aircraft, ammunition – were desperately lacking.

Thus, when Barbarossa began to lose momentum despite its intoxicating early triumphs, the supply situation for the German army and for the Luftwaffe deteriorated rapidly. With the coming of winter and the absolute lack of specialized clothing and equipment, Hitler's forces found

11

themselves plunged into miseries more terrible than those endured by the British Army in the Crimea a century earlier, and incomparably worse in scale. Vehicle engines seized, guns froze, aircraft became useless, men were driven to clothe themselves in layers of newspapers beneath their tunics in the pitiful struggle to save themselves from the cold. The Red Army also suffered greatly, but it was fighting in its own element. By that winter, even those in London and Washington who had anticipated a speedy Russian collapse cherished growing hopes that in the East, at last, Hitler's manic ambitions were foundering.

It is impossible to overstate the influence of Germany's huge commitment in Russia upon other theatres of war. In the Libyan desert the British were only narrowly holding their own against the Italians and a German Afrika Korps of barely two divisions. A reinforcement of a few German formations, a fraction of the force in the East, would almost certainly have proved decisive in enabling Rommel to reach Cairo and occupy the entire Mediterranean littoral. Yet Hitler could not spare these.

Throughout the years of war that remained, the German strategic imperative remained constant: the East consumed the vast bulk of manpower and industrial output. Hitler grudged every man and gun dispatched to other theatres. He conceded to his commanders only the bare minimum of resources to avoid catastrophe in North Africa and later Italy. The East dominated his thoughts and his fears, and soon his nightmares. The knowledge of the terrible revenge that Russia would exact for Germany's cruelties, the understanding of the price of defeat, weighed upon every German soldier and airman on the battlefield. In the East, on 22 June 1941 Hitler had loosed forces utterly beyond his powers to control, and changed the face of the world at least for the balance of the twentieth century.

The photographs in this book in some ways belie the nature of the Russo–German war, for they give little hint of its absolute horror. They provide fascinating glimpses of the face of the German army at war, of a technical quality most uncommon among the colour pictures of the period. Because they cover only the early stages of the campaign, they suggest the sunshine naïvety that imbued so many of Hitler's men, flushed with victory, in those first months in Russia. Disenchantment, despair,

12

and final disaster lay ahead. But in all the wars of the twentieth century, there have been more photographers at hand to record the moments of advance and of victory than those of retreat and catastrophe of the kind which the *Wehrmacht* was to endure in the East from 1942 to 1945.

Max Hastings

Guilsborough Lodge
Northamptonshire
April 1984

The German Drive
to Stalingrad

Prelude

The declaration of war by Germany at dawn on 22 June 1941, and the simultaneous invasion of the Soviet Union by the *Wehrmacht*, brought to an end twenty-five years of peaceful German–Soviet relations. This 'peace' had included perfidious acts on both sides, as well as the occasional spell of collaboration.

Imperial German backing for the Bolshevik revolution had, of course, been anything but altruistic. The Bolsheviks were heavily financed by the Germans in the hope of hastening Russia's collapse. The government even allowed Lenin and four hundred other revolutionaries to enter Russia through Germany in 1917. But the young Soviet state had to pay for this with the Treaty of Brest Litovsk in 1918, whose provisions came close to meeting Hitler's later visions of a German colonial empire in the East.

In the end, however, it all rebounded on the prime movers. The germs of revolution they had helped to sow infected the German people who, like the Russians, had had quite enough of hunger and war. The Kaiser had to seek asylum abroad, and his generals to call off the war they had lost. The Bolsheviks exploited the unrest by exporting their version of the revolution to Germany, thus forcing the ruling Social Democrats to enlist the aid of the Kaiser's generals, men they had only just thrown over – a birth trauma from which the newly born German Republic was never to recover.

Soon afterwards the two big losers of the First World War, the Weimar Republic and the Soviet Union, discovered interests in common. Thanks to the 1922 Treaty of Rapallo they not only improved their position towards the victors of Versailles but also agreed on close military collaboration – not, of course, without ulterior motives on both sides. The *Reichswehr* and the Red Army alike made good use of the secret German bases in the Soviet Union where tanks, heavy artillery and aircraft were developed and tested in defiance of the Treaty of Versailles. Soviet

17

officers took cramming courses at the German Military Academy even as the Red Army taught German communists the tactics of civil war. In the late twenties, when General von Blomberg, later Hitler's Minister of War, went to the Soviet Union to inspect the *Reichswehr* bases, the Kharkov Soviet mistook him for Max Hölz, leader of a petty uprising in Vogtland whom communist propaganda had blown up into a general. They welcomed the bemused Blomberg as a hero of the German proletariat, with a guard of honour, the *Internationale* (the national anthem of the Soviet Union until 1944) and all – a small slip in the game of intrigue played out behind the back of both nations which was later to be followed by others far more ominous.

Hitler first denounced the cynical alliance with the Soviet Union in *Mein Kampf* (1925). When he wrote the book he had no inkling, of course, how much he himself would benefit from that alliance: on his seizure of power he was able to avail himself of ready-made cadre units for his panzer divisions and his air force. To him, the Bolshevik revolution was the hand of fate; he believed that the vast empire in the East was on the point of collapse because the Jews had eliminated its Nordic élite, which alone was fit to govern. Germany must be a world power or nothing at all, he proclaimed. *Lebensraum*, living space to be tilled by the German plough, would have to be wrested with the sword from the inferior Slavs on the soil of the Soviet Union. That was the central thread of his philosophy, to which he subordinated everything else.

It is considered chic these days to call Hitler a 'leftist', a kind of radical socialist, or even a vague social democrat. But what justification is there for these views? When all is said and done, Hitler's ambitions were nothing but the pipe dreams of a pan-Germanic imperialist spiced with fanatical hatred of the Jews and carried to excess. Hitler knew right from left far better than his modern interpreters. Everybody to the left of the German National People's Party – democrats, socialists, communists, pacifists and trade unionists – was an enemy to be eradicated if Hitler was to realize his ambitions. The authoritarian and monolithic state that emerged as a result was entirely to the liking of the German 'right', the more so as Hitler never showed any signs of wanting to overturn the old power structures in government, industry or the army. His method was to coax them into line very gently while making use of their administrative skills which, as a rule, they were only too happy to proffer. Such sops to social equality as 'Strength through Joy', single-course Sunday dinners, and the abolition of separate entrances for tradesmen, were concessions the right could readily accept. After all, they remained masters in their own houses – or so at least they thought. By the time they discovered their mistake it was too late.

The heads of the *Reichswehr* (armed forces) were a special case. They, who as officers of the Kaiser had seen fit to withhold sergeant's stripes from Hitler on the grounds that he lacked leadership potential, were the only men he feared, for they held real power. To forge his sword he had to have their loyal and active collaboration. And so he paid court to them, granted them all the privileges due to the 'nation's only shield' and even sacrificed some of his overambitious and power-hungry comrades-in-arms who wished to challenge these privileges because they did not grasp his long-term objectives. His reward was immediate: like the Kaiser before him, he had his generals swear an oath of allegiance to his person. That a few of their old cronies lost their lives during the so-called *Röhm putsch* in 1934 when a large number of prominent Nazis suspected of less than complete loyalty to the Führer (including Ernst Röhm, then head of the Storm troops) were eliminated) was, of course, a matter for regret, but only caused a brief flurry. 'You cannot make an omelette without breaking eggs' was a saying on many people's lips after 30 June 1934. And everyone seemed to agree with Hitler that there was a need for omelettes.

The generals' initial reservations about the corporal soon made way for growing admiration. Just look at how the fellow tackled things – the way he had cast off the chains of Versailles, restored the Reich's military sovereignty, and speeded the annexation of Austria in March 1938 – like some dashing guards officer but with infallible tactical skill as well, and a sure sense of time and place.

It is true that some of the more level-headed of the old élite found Hitler's tempo a little too fast and furious. Naturally, they had no objections in principle to the dismantling of Czechoslovakia, that 'French aircraft carrier' lying right in the middle of German territory. But would the Western powers stand for it without going to war? Would it not be better to overthrow the adventurer before he recklessly gambled away what had only just been won?

19

But again Hitler was proved right. Britain and France dropped their Czech ally without scruple, delivering Sudetenland to Hitler in the autumn of 1938 and with it the Czech border fortifications. Now he was in a position to step up the tempo even further.

He sent the prophets of gloom and the defeatists, who had been given the lie by the West's capitulation at Munich and were now utterly discredited, into the wilderness, pocketed the rest of Czechoslovakia and rounded on Poland. If the Western Powers had abandoned Czechoslovakia, he argued, there was no reason why they should stand up and be counted for Poland. 'All my actions are aimed at Russia,' he told a foreign visitor in Berchtesgaden. 'If the West is too stupid to realize that, I shall have to come to terms with Russia, beat the West and then attack Russia with redoubled strength.'

Terms with Russia? Terms between Hitler, the 'butcher of the workers', and Stalin, the 'bloodhound of international Jewish Bolshevism', as they called each other? Hitler's visitor, Carl Jacob Burckhardt, the League of Nations High Commissioner in the Free City of Danzig, considered this announcement so absurd that he did not even mention it in his official report to Western diplomats. In the event, however, just such an understanding was about to be reached. The question whether or not Hitler could still be stopped suddenly depended on whether Stalin would fall in with Hitler's offer to share Poland with him, or, more precisely, on whether Stalin still had other options.

Stalin had just come through ten years of bloody civil war. In the process, millions of farms and smallholdings had been collectivized, millions of peasants and their families had been liquidated and millions of others had starved to death. This had been followed by a veritable holocaust of 'purges' among leaders of the state, the party and industry, and finally by the decapitation of the Red Army. According to Soviet sources, purges of the army alone had cost the lives of between three to five Marshals of the Soviet Union, all the district and divisional commanders, nearly all the brigade-generals and half the regimental commanders – all in all, at least 30,000 senior officers. And now the West expected Stalin, the man who had waded ankle deep in the blood of his subjects for a decade, to pull their chestnuts out of the fire into which they had allowed them to drop in Munich in 1938. But how? With a leaderless army and with the Japanese hard at his heels on the Amur river? And for the sake of the Poles, who clearly preferred being overrun by the Germans to being rescued by the Red Army? (One can sympathize with them – Stalin was the devil they knew, while Hitler's crimes were only to be guessed at.) On the other hand, could he sit back and look on, just as the Western Powers were bound to sit back and look on, while Hitler swallowed Poland whole and so advanced his potential marshalling area as far as Minsk and Kamenets Podolskiy, or even through the Baltic as far as Narva? Should he, perhaps, since Poland was in any case past saving, at least seize that part of the doomed country Hitler was prepared to hand over to him as a kind of insurance policy? He would be gaining territory and time, both of which the West had surrendered at Munich, but which Soviet Russia would badly need in 1941. He chose the last gambit, which, of all the bad moves left to him in this hopelessly confused game of international chess, was undoubtedly the strongest. Indeed, if we look at the 1941 campaign it was perhaps decisive.

Meanwhile he kept a careful eye on the Western Powers to see if they would actually fight the war they had declared on Hitler following his invasion of Poland. Only when, at the beginning of September 1939, it had become clear that the French had no intention of coming to the aid of their Polish ally with an offensive in the West, where at the time they were vastly superior to the Germans, did Stalin move: only then, and not a day sooner. In the event, the breathing space he gained through this shameful bargain was small. But who could have foreseen how quickly and dearly the French would be made to pay for their betrayal of Poland?

Hitler's lightning victory over France in May–June 1940 meant that nearly all the conditions for victory in the East he had first set out in *Mein Kampf* had been met. All he had failed to achieve was an alliance with Britain. Hess flew to Scotland to remedy this slight defect, to no avail. Hitler was unconcerned. The British Army had been driven from the Continent, and for years to come there could be no threat to him from a second front in the West. Now he could at last instruct his generals to work out a plan of campaign against the Soviet Union.

In many accounts of the Second World War we are told that Hitler did not turn against the East until it became clear that Goering's *Luftwaffe* could not gain air supremacy over Britain, thus rendering the proposed

German landing in England, code-named 'Sea Lion', impossible. In fact, however, Hitler did not even wait for the beginning, let alone the outcome, of Göring's air offensive when he decided that in the following year, 1941, that he would destroy the Soviet Union. His Chief of Staff, General Franz Halder, made shorthand notes of what Hitler told his generals as early as 31 July 1940, well before 'Eagle Day', which introduced the full-scale aerial offensive of the *Luftwaffe* against Britain. 'Britain's hope lies in Russia and America,' Hitler said. 'If that hope in Russia is destroyed, then the hope in America will have been destroyed as well, because the elimination of Russia will enormously increase Japan's power in the Far East. Decision: Russia must be liquidated. The sooner the better. Operation pointless unless Soviet state smashed in one fell swoop. Territorial gains alone not enough. Aim: destruction of Russia's vital strength. Beginning of campaign: May 1941. Five months to finish it.'

The German people had no inkling of what was being planned for them. 'At last we've finally done it,' they thought. What more could possibly be asked of them? Germany was the leading power in Europe. It might prove difficult to consolidate and safeguard recent gains, but surely it was possible to use this new position of strength to make peace with the nations of Europe, just as Bismarck had seen fit to do following his great victories. To seek even more power, even more glorious victories, even more territory, would surely be tempting the gods.

What Hitler now planned burst the bounds of all recorded history. A major European power was to be wiped off the face of the earth, its vital strength destroyed. To that end, its people would have to be partly eradicated, partly driven beyond the Urals, and partly used as high-class beasts of burden. According to computations by a team of German economists, twenty to thirty million people would have to starve to death if the assault was to be worthwhile. International law and those principles of chivalry on which the German soldier so prided himself were to be set aside. With this adventure Germany thus withdrew from the community of civilized nations and surrendered every right ever again to be judged by the tenets of international law. Even if it ended in victory, the exploit was bound, ultimately, to bring about Germany's downfall – the rest of the world would have no option but to join forces and work for the destruction of a country run amok.

One might have thought that Hitler's demented dreams of empire would have so thoroughly alarmed the old German establishment – which, after all, still wielded considerable power in the armed forces – that it would by now have closed ranks to prevent this suicidal destruction of the German Reich. But oddly enough, resistance was remarkably weak, half-hearted and sporadic – far more so than it had been to any of Hitler's earlier ventures. Plainly Hitler's onslaught, because it was directed against the Bolsheviks, was seen as an attack on some lawless jungle, a moral vacuum, predestined to be peopled with German supermen. Had not the Kaiser, too, anticipating Hitler, exclaimed in 1918, at the last meeting of his Crown Council: 'Bolsheviks? The Jewish revenge! The whole lot should be wiped out!' And just that was about to take place, and what was uppermost in the minds of the men in charge of the preparations was not the question of right and wrong but of expediency. Moral scruples were confined to a small minority, without influence or power.

The German soldiers who, in 1941, massed along the borders of the Soviet Union, did not realize what was being done in their name. They trusted their officers who would not, they were sure, have ordered this desperate attack unless the need was extreme. True, some may have dreamt of a farm alongside the Dnieper or of an estate on the shores of the Black Sea, and many may even have believed in the superiority of the German race or been taken in by the slogan: 'The Russians must die so that we may live.' The great majority, however, were simply obeying orders, certain in the belief that 'those at the top' knew their business. This appears to be a besetting weakness of all nations, one to which, paradoxically, they succumb the more readily the less 'those at the top' do in fact know what they are doing.

'Whom the gods wish to destroy, they first strike blind.' On 22 June 1941, however, the gods had thought up something altogether special: they struck two parties at once with blindness, then leant back in their seats and laid bets on which of the two blind fools about to turn on each other would come out on top. For that was far from certain at the outset.

23

The Campaign

On Sunday, 15 June 1941, rumour was rife in Berlin that the Soviet Union was in for a surprise in a week's time. That same day, Richard Sorge, the Tokyo correspondent of the *Frankfurter Zeitung* and a secret communist agent, sent a radio signal to Moscow: 'War will start on 22 June.' To Stalin this was just another of the 'dubious and misleading reports' by which Sorge had been warning Moscow of the impending attack for the past four months. English warnings, too, he dismissed as so many dirty tricks aimed at forcing him into a general mobilization, and as a result into a war with Hitler. That was something he was determined to put off for as long as he could, so little confidence did he have in his own country's powers of resistance. Only a few hours before the first German shells burst, he had instructed Molotov, his foreign minister, to ask the German ambassador whether the German government had any cause for complaint, and if so what could be done to improve relations. Stalin was ready to make Hitler any concessions he asked. A German communist who deserted and crossed the River Bug on 21 June 1941 to warn his comrades of the impending onslaught was put against the wall and shot as an *agent provocateur*.

We can only speculate on Stalin's reasons for refusing so obstinately to face the facts. Trust in Hitler's promises cannot have been the answer, for trust was foreign to Stalin's nature. Nor was it complacency, since fear of Hitler had stamped Soviet politics ever since 1938. We can only assume that Stalin, despite – or indeed because of – the purges of the Red Army, went so much in fear of his own soldiers that he dared not mobilize them until the very moment of a German attack, an emergency that would unite his people and circumvent any chances of a military uprising against him.

Thanks to Stalin's cowardliness, therefore, the Red Army was taken completely by surprise when the Germans struck. A large part of the Red Air Force was destroyed on the ground where it stood, without fuel and in review order. German panzer spearheads tore deep into Soviet territory like so many bullets, scattering Red Army units in all directions. However bravely and loyally they resisted, in the prevailing chaos the defenders were fighting a losing battle. Their commanding officers, most of them creatures of Stalin's purges – that is, a random selection of obsequious and incompetent yes-men – proved hopeless in a situation that called for independent judgement and resolve. The upshot was panic: hundreds of thousands of Soviet soldiers deserted or surrendered at the first opportunity. They were mostly peasant lads, who had not forgotten the horrors of forced collectivization and saw little reason to fight and die for Stalin.

The three and a half million or so German soldiers and their allies who attacked with 3,700 tanks (only 800 more than had been used in France) and 2,700 aircraft, were opposed by five million Red Army men (though at first only half of these were deployed on Russia's western borders), 15,000, mainly antiquated, tanks and 8,000 aircraft, of which even the most modern, some 800, were no technical match for the *Luftwaffe*. All in all, however, this was an army that, had it been mobilized in time and led by capable generals, would have been able to halt the German invasion within the first few weeks.

But what was it Marshal Budënny had said to a comrade in the days of the great purges? 'Don't be afraid, they won't be coming for the fools.' And indeed Stalin liquidated not the fools but only the best of his officers, especially those trained by the Germans. Now, with few exceptions, the Red Army was indeed led mostly by fools: by three Civil War veterans who knew next to nothing about modern warfare, and by Stalin's minions from the secret police and the party. They were military novices whose main instrument of command was the art of passing the buck. In these circumstances, the only two men with a solid military background in the upper echelons of the Red Army, Zhukov, who had distinguished himself against the Japanese, and Shaposhnikov, once the youngest colonel in the Tsar's army, could do little to save the situation. Ruined lines of communication, combined with the rapid and reckless advances of German panzer units made it almost impossible to co-ordinate the actions of the shattered ranks of the Red Army. Small wonder, then, that the Red Army lost more than three million prisoners of war within a mere four months, as well as an unknown number of casualties that must certainly have run into millions, and 10,000 tanks and 15,000 field guns. What country on earth could have borne such losses? But as a shrewd Soviet critic recently pointed out, it was thanks to the paradoxical dialectics of world history that the very Stalinist methods that had led to these defeats also proved the means for reversing them.

For despite their victories, unprecedented in history, the German advance failed to reach its set objectives. This was due not only to the unusually dogged fight put up by sections of the Red Army, but even more importantly to the very nearly insurmountable difficulties of keeping the German lines of supply open. At last the territory and the time Stalin had gained in 1939 began to pay dividends. Brand-new weapons that had been produced over the past eighteen months suddenly appeared: the notorious 'Stalin organ' (a multiple rocket launcher) and, in particular, the T–34 tank, which was superior to most German panzers both in armour and manoeuvrability and which was to become the main instrument of the later Soviet victories. Frequent downpours transformed the so-called roads of the western Soviet Union into impassable rivers of mud in which the German wheeled vehicles became bogged down. Entire German panzer divisions, some stretched out over more than ninety miles, were often immobilized by lack of fuel. In dry weather, by contrast, the non-motorized divisions, which accounted for more than three-quarters of the German forces in the East, could not keep up with the panzer formations despite superhuman marches. As a consequence, the pincers round the Soviet armies could not be closed quickly enough, so that time and again large numbers of men were able to escape to the East. Even so, two weeks after the onslaught Hitler and Halder were firmly convinced that the 'Eastern Campaign' was as good as won. World public opinion shared this view, London and Washington giving the Soviet Union three months at most to total collapse.

But now Hitler was to repay Stalin for services rendered. He forgot what any young reader of his favourite German adventure-story writer, Karl May, could have told him: make sure a bear is dead before you skin it. At the end of July 1941, after more than five weeks of continuous and bitter fighting, the losses, wear and tear and supply problems of Army Group Centre – whose commanding officer, Field Marshal von Bock, already saw himself in the role of conqueror of Moscow – imposed a breathing space. Hitler decided that it was time to pick up some spoils of war. The Ukraine, granary of the Soviet Union, the coal mines and factories of the Donets Basin, and the treasures of Leningrad all enticed him. And so he detailed the tanks of Army Group Centre to the flanks, moving them against Leningrad, which was to elude him, and into the Ukraine, where the Germans took nearly 700,000 prisoners. But Kiev was not Moscow, that political hub at which all the spokes of the Stalinist power machine came together. The loss of Moscow would have been a terrible blow to the Soviet Union, resulting in considerable damage to the centrifugal forces of this multinational state. Strategically, too, Moscow was a particularly worthwhile objective, for it was the main traffic junction of western Russia, the great railway turntable through which nearly all Red Army supplies passed and were distributed. The encircle-ment of Moscow would have split the Red Army into two, with inestim-able effects on the overall situation.

On 30 September 1941, Army Group Centre prepared to smash the assembled Soviet Fronts (comparable to German Army Groups) outside Moscow in the double battle of Vyazma and Bryansk. According to the objectives of Operation Barbarossa, this attack ought to have been launched as early as 2 August, and in fact, but for Hitler's interference, it could have begun in the middle of August. But by the end of September the chances of success had evaporated. True, the West Front near Vyazma, the Bryansk Front and to some extent also the Reserve Front to the rear of the other two, were almost completely encircled and wiped out, but the Germans could no longer exploit this tremendous victory to the full because the rainy season and the mud it produced slowed down their offensive and finally brought it to a halt. Zhukov, who was to round on his party bosses after the war with 'You did not send our troops into battle but to slaughter', had time to drum up another 200,000 men and to improvise a new line of defence. With the onset of the frosts the German divisions made one last desperate attempt to encircle Moscow, but now Zhukov's men managed to stave off the bloodied, burned-out and exhausted enemy troops until the unusually harsh and early winter, with temperatures of down to minus 30°C, overtook the German soldiers, most of them still in summer uniform.

In the North, the Germans had advanced to within 12 miles of Moscow, in the West to within 30 miles and in the South, pushing on from Tula, to

27

within 60 miles. It is not hard to imagine what would have happened had Hitler not postponed the offensive against Moscow for six weeks, or if the Germans had started the onslaught on 22 June not from Brest-Litovsk but from Minsk. For in that case, Hitler would probably not have made his grave strategic error at the end of July; had he been some 120 miles nearer to Moscow he would not have given orders to go for the spoils of war and Moscow could have been encircled as early as October. What that might have meant is of course mere speculation, but Stalin later confessed that even as it was his fate had hung by a thread. Soviet generals spoke of a second 'miracle of the Marne' and Zhukov called the battle for Moscow the decisive battle of the whole war. From this we may probably take it, without stretching the imagination too far, that the collapse of Moscow would probably have led to the collapse of the Soviet Union.

Hitler also lent Stalin further crucial assistance when, confident that victory was assured, he prematurely let slip the mask the German propaganda machinery had made him put on: that of Hitler the Liberator. To start with, German soldiers had been welcomed as saviours in many parts of the Soviet Union. The fighting spirit of many a Red Army man had left much to be desired, and who could blame them after what Stalin had done to their country? But very quickly the news was out that the Germans were, if anything, worse. Nearly two million of their three million prisoners of war were left by them to die miserably in the open, generally in full view of the population. As a German general explained, that was the best – because it was the quietest – method of getting rid of the Slav rabble. Hard on the heels of the German troops followed the SS murder squads and a civil administration led by fanatical Nazis, both groups making it abundantly clear in the shortest possible time that things were to be far more murderous under them than under Stalin. Not surprisingly, Stalin's call for a 'Great Patriotic War' on 3 July 1941, when he had finally recovered from the shock of 22 June, fell on fertile soil. Red Army resolve hardened from week to week. The first partisan units made their presence felt to the rear of the *Wehrmacht*, sabotaging German lines of supply. The inhabitants of the Soviet Union had been left with no alternative but to fight for dear life, and hence for Stalin.

Thus, by his onslaught on the Soviet Union, Hitler worked three miracles at once (not counting the 'miracle of the Marne' before the gates of Moscow): he turned irreconcilable enemies, the Soviet Union and the Anglo-Saxons, into allies; he transformed recalcitrant and sullen subjects into Soviet patriots; and he finally persuaded people throughout the world to look upon the Soviet Union as the last bulwark of freedom. Those gods thirsting for human sacrifices who had laid their bets on Stalin were about to pick up their winnings. Ten million dead had been delivered, another twenty million were to follow.

The Defeat

On 15 October 1941, two weeks after Hitler ordered the resumption of the offensive against Moscow, Richard Sorge sent a signal from Tokyo saying that Japan no longer posed a threat to the USSR in the Far East. Japan, her oil tap firmly turned off by the USA, could not possibly join in the war against the Soviet Union; if she did not want to give up her imperialist plans, she would now have to look to the Pacific. This time Stalin believed the German master spy; he withdrew his battle-tested Siberian divisions, trained to cope with the toughest climatic conditions and equipped accordingly, from the Manchurian border and sent them to the West. The first contingents arrived only just in time to take part in the relief of Moscow. The rest, the great majority, mounted a counter-offensive against the German Army Group Centre, which now had suddenly to fight for dear life instead of moving into the comfortable winter quarters in Moscow the German High Command had assigned to them just a few weeks earlier.

Which of us today can still put himself in the place of those who, at temperatures of 18, 25, 36°C below zero, were forced day after day, night after night, to advance, retreat, attack and flee, on icy, snow-bound roads, over fields and frozen bogs, knee-deep in snow, through villages burnt to the ground, when gunlocks refused to budge, engines refused to start, and machine-guns refused to fire; when skin stuck in shreds to the steel of weapons and utensils, and legs in army boots were as cold as the snow and the ice? With a remorseless foe in hot pursuit, the Red Army was fuelled by an icy hatred of Nazi brutality, and a determination to recapture the villages laid waste by war. What the men on both sides went through during those four winter months defies all description. In the month of January 1942, the German Army lost 150,000 men – twelve divisions – through frost and illness on the Eastern Front.

The claim is now heard that at the time Hitler saved the Eastern Front from total collapse by his orders to hang on at any price, in the face of all tactical considerations. The truth is that these orders cost the lives of tens of thousands more men. Beyond that they enabled the Red Army, which had simply intended to push the Germans as far back from Moscow as possible, to trap twelve enemy divisions at Demyansk. The Eastern Front held, not because of Hitler's orders, but simply because the German soldier had developed a capacity for suffering not unlike the Russian's. Hitler's orders merely proved that the 'Führer' had reached the end of his tether, that he had lost the war. The time limit he had set himself – five months – had long since passed. His plan to smash the Soviet Union in one fell swoop had misfired. Russia had not been 'eliminated', nor had the United States, despite the 'enormous increase of Japan's power'. On the contrary, the treacherous Japanese attack on Pearl Harbour had merely served to bring the United States into the war officially. When Hitler grandiloquently declared war on the USA on 11 December 1941, he knew he had nothing more to lose – he simply wanted to deflect attention from his defeat in Moscow. At about the same time, the so-called Wannsee Conference decided on the perfection of methods of mass murder, for at least this much the failed would-be conqueror could still achieve: the extermination of the Jews as an integral part of his racist dreams of world domination.

Today, even those who lived through the period can barely understand why the German people failed to realize that the war had been irretrievably lost. 'Raise high your nose and firmly close your eyes,' cynics sang to the tune of the Nazis' *Horst Wessel* song ('Raise high the flag and firmly close your ranks'). Others coined the slogan: 'Enjoy the war, the peace will be much worse.'

But the masses continued to believe in final victory. Hitler, having learnt the lesson of 1918, had eradicated every potential leader of a revolt. And there was no hope of resistance from below as the people lulled themselves with the promise of miracle weapons, or with hopes of a split between the Allies (who, in fact, now that the survival of the Soviet Union was no longer in the balance, joined in closer collaboration). Some even continued to believe that an alliance between Germany and the Western Allies against the Soviet Union was still a possibility. Nothing was too fantastic to be disbelieved.

The desperate predicament of the ordinary German soldier was recorded in his diary by a young cadet officer, just before he was killed: 'It is often extremely difficult to carry out orders. We have just had to raze an entire village to the ground. The poor people! "You're supposed to be a cultured nation," a woman said to me. All one can do is shrug one's shoulders. They begged us on their bended knees, offered us all their money, held out their icons to us. But what good was that? Orders are orders. For what terrible crimes are we being punished, even in our youth? Who is it all for? Is the war a big swindle after all? Why do we put up with it all? For the Führer, the nation, the fatherland? No! No! No! We put up with it just because our comrades are in the shit with us and we can't leave them in it. They've got to put a stop to this slaughter of young people, now, while there is still time. But that lot has no conscience. That's all – the Russians are attacking – farewell! It will soon be over!'

The bitterest deaths were not those of men who still believed in the Führer, in victory and the 'cause', but of those who had come to realize with what lack of scruple they were being misused and sacrificed. 'They are too sacred to answer for their actions.' This young man understood what the truth of the matter would turn out to be.

Much ink has been spilled since the war on the reasons for Germany's suicidal perseverance right up to 8 May 1945. Fear of the Bolsheviks, Red Army atrocities, the gospel of hatred preached by the propagandist Ilya Ehrenburg, the Allies' demand for unconditional surrender, Goebbels's propaganda – all of them more or less applied. However, the strongest motive of all – the fear of having to answer for what they did to other people in general, and the Soviet people in particular, for, with and under Hitler – that motive has been, and continues to be, largely denied and ignored. The German people were filled with a secret horror of what would happen if Germany lost the war, a campaign of pillage and destruction unequalled in the annals of history. It was not just 'those at the top' who were afraid of the reckoning. The whole nation had the feeling that it had burned its bridges and could expect neither mercy nor pity. It was not the war crimes of their enemies (which were often no more than self-defence carried to extremes), but their own bad consciences for the ghastly crimes committed by the Nazis in their name that were the deepest and surest foundations of the German 'faith in final victory', a faith that flew in the fact of every kind of political and military logic.

Stalingrad

If Hitler ever had a chance of bringing the Soviet Union to her knees, that chance was lost before Moscow. Yet in the summer of 1942, when the *Wehrmacht* once more seized the initiative, and after the capture of Sebastopol and the rout of Marshal Timoshenko's armies – which had massed near Kharkov in May for the recapture of the Ukraine – went over to the offensive, advancing to the Volga and the edge of the Caucasus, the world again held its breath. Would the Soviet Union collapse after all? For one hundred days both armies fought for Stalingrad with ferocious intensity. During those hundred days, the Soviets prepared a classical *retour offensif* against the hopelessly overstretched German lines; their incredible objective was to cut off and rout no less than two German Army Groups, in the Caucasus and at Stalingrad. To that end, the Red Army struck out from points north and south of Stalingrad on the night of 18 November, and within a few days had trapped the German Sixth Army with more than twenty-two divisions and at least 300,000 men in a 'pocket' between the Volga and the Don.

From General von Weichs, Commander of Army Group B, through General Paulus, Commander of the Sixth Army, down to the divisional commanders in the pocket, everyone was agreed that only a quick break-out could now save the situation. Hitler nevertheless ordered the army to adopt a 'hedgehog' (i.e., all-round defensive) position outside Stalingrad. The troops would be supplied from the air and could count on speedy relief.

At this point, the German generals did not need higher powers of political and moral judgement but quite simply a sense of responsibility. Since they were all agreed that a break-out attempt was the only way out of the impasse, they had simply to do what they knew was right. There need have been no question of a conspiracy or insubordination. For even the youngest cadet officer learns at the military academy that he cannot be expected to follow patently absurd orders, indeed must not follow orders he considers absurd. What was needed was simply an appeal to that oft-invoked *esprit de corps* of the German officer, to his professional pride and to what Clausewitz (the Prussian general and military theorist) called his 'guild spirit', by which he wanted to stress that the soldier's job is first of all a trade. The soldier does not, however, deal in leather, iron, flour, wood or cotton, but in human lives, which obliges him to follow the rules of his trade with particular care – in his field, bungled work turns into crime very quickly.

A simple, apolitical general, General von Seydlitz, who until then had had little more objection to Hitler than that he wore a badly fitting uniform and that he had committed tactical errors at Demyansk, explained on 25 November 1942 from inside the Stalingrad pocket – that is, from on the spot and not after long armchair deliberations – what the duty of honest tradesmen would have been at the time (see Appendix: Documents). After an expert analysis of the situation, fully confirmed by the subsequent course of events, he told his comrades and superiors: 'Unless the Army High Command revokes the order to hold the hedgehog position immediately, my own conscience and responsibility to the Army and the German people impose the imperative duty to seize the freedom of action curtailed by the previous order and to use what little time is left to avoid utter disaster by a break-out attempt.' All that was needed was agreement between General Paulus and Field Marshal von Manstein, who had taken command of Weich's Army Group, and the determination of both men, regardless of the hysterical clamour raised by a Führer safe in his 'Wolf's Lair', to do what the rules of their trade demanded.

One is of course entitled to ask what good it would have done had the Sixth Army been saved against Hitler's will. Would it not, like the rest of the *Wehmacht*, have been destroyed in some other place? Possibly so. However, it is also possible that such an act of overt defiance by an entire Army Group, such an act of revolt against the arrogant exactions of a dictator, might have changed the whole attitude of the *Wehrmacht* High Command. Had the generals seized this unique opportunity of driving home to the dictator, in so dramatic a fashion, where the limits of his power lay, had Hitler's continued hold on his generals been broken for once, then he would most certainly have been unable to turn the whole of Germany into a superdimensional Stalingrad.

General von Seydlitz's courageous memorandum was transmitted by
the Sixth Army (whose Chief of Staff, General Arthur Schmidt, wrote in
the margin: 'We don't have to cudgel the Führer's brains. . .!) to Army
Group B, where it was put on one side and forgotten.

General von Seydlitz's action has been played down on the grounds
that, as commander of the northern front of the Stalingrad pocket, he was
directly responsible to Hitler and could therefore have acted on his own
initiative had he really been brave enough to defy Hitler's orders. But this
objection is quite absurd. It was impossible for one part of the pocket –
least of all the northern front – to break out alone; the entire Sixth Army
had to be involved and, moreover, in co-ordination with a relief operation
mounted from the outside. All Seydlitz could hope to do was to drive
home to his superiors and to his comrades where to draw the line on
military discipline and, if necessary, he could then have capitulated on his
own in January. But even then, although he enjoyed their highest respect,
his men might not have followed him – not yet. Manstein and Paulus, for
their part, allowed themselves to be taken in by quite blatantly absurd
promises of supplies by air and reinforcements on the ground. Seydlitz
had calculated that his LI Corps, consisting of eight divisions, i.e. a good
third of the Sixth Army, needed 590 to 990 tons of supplies a day, on a
conservative estimate. A division readily uses up 100 tons of ammunition
in one day of major battle. The daily ration issued to the German soldier
today weighs about 1.5kg, which for the 300,000 men in the pocket would
have added up to 450 tons of provisions alone. In addition there was the
fodder for the horses, and fuel for the distribution of the provisions and
ammunition and to move the heavy guns and tanks – all in all, between
1,600 and 2,600 tons for the entire encircled Sixth Army. But the Sixth
Army Command thought it could manage with a mere 700 tons. Army
Group B made a further reduction of more than 30 per cent with the claim
that 450 tons would be sufficient; in the end, the OKH (the *Wehrmacht*
High Command) asked Goering to fly in at least 300 tons a day, thus
misleading the latter into making his first grandiloquent claims of being
able to supply the Sixth Army from the air. As it was, less than 100 tons a
day was in fact airlifted into the pocket, something any *Luftwaffe*
squadron leader could have predicted. As for the promised reinforcements, von Manstein was able to muster a total of one whole and two half

panzer divisions. Had they broken into the pocket they would surely have been trapped together with the Sixth Army; moreover, the reserves needed to protect the 90-mile long corridor into the pocket against flanking attacks by the Red Army were simply not available. By the time the panzer divisions had approached to within 30 miles of the pocket, the Sixth Army, as von Seydlitz had predicted, no longer had the strength to advance towards them. The fate of the Sixth Army was sealed.

However, they were ordered to fight on as long as provisions and ammunition lasted, with the aim of tying down the greatest possible enemy concentration. For in the meantime the entire German front on the Don, as far north as Voronezh, had collapsed and all the Germans could now hope to do militarily was to 'contain the defeat', as von Manstein put it. In similar circumstances at Vyazma, the enemy had fought on, tying down the Germans until Zhukov was able to build up a new line of defence that played a crucial role in the relief of Moscow.

But by Christmas 1942, deaths in the pocket from malnutrition, hypothermia and overexertion were rapidly multiplying. A pathologist was flown in to examine the casualties and one of his post-mortems reads as follows: 'Very little adipose tissue beneath the skin and surrounding the internal organs. Gelatinous fluid in the mesentery. Organs very pale. Red and yellow bone marrow replaced by vitreous substance. Liver congested; heart muscle atrophied; right ventricle and right auricle greatly enlarged.' Could it really be asked of soldiers that they continue fighting in this condition? After the war, von Manstein described the Red Army's stubborn defence of Sebastopol as a 'prime example of that contempt for human life elevated into a principle by an Asiatic power'. Here in Stalingrad it was to become clear how much respect for human life the Prussian, Christian, European generals had for the 300,000 German soldiers entrusted to their care. The Sixth Army starved to death. At least 30,000 wounded men were left lying, virtually unattended, in the cellars of the ruined city. Typhus, typhoid, dysentery, cholera, jaundice and malaria were rife. There was hardly any ammunition. Heavy guns could not be moved. The Sixth Army had performed truly superhuman feats and suffered superhuman agonies. No military, no human law could ask any more of them. On 10 January 1943, the Red Army sent a surrender ultimatum. Could the Germans dare refuse? Or the generals dare to make

36

their men pay even more for their leaders' blunders? Indeed they could. Remorselessly they drove the starving, the wounded, the prematurely aged and debilitated into further battle under threat of capital punishment (and 364 actual executions). Their men were expected to face the Soviet T-34s with knives and bared teeth – and this was demanded of them by the man who had not wanted to cudgel the Führer's brains but who himself asked to be flown out at the last moment.

And so the Red Army struck, squashing the pocket like a metal-crusher. Soviet tanks simply ground the defenceless German infantry into the frozen earth. Medical and food supplies were cut off from those wounded who were no longer able even to crawl and who had become expendable, and the Red Army moved in with flame-throwers and Molotov cocktails to clear out the cellars in which these wretches lay. Then the T–34s drew up before the bunkers and cellars of the generals. There had originally been thirty-four generals in the pocket. Seven had been flown out, including one who was wounded. One had gone missing, another had chosen suicide, and just one had sought and found death on the battlefield. The rest were quick to despatch radio messages crackling with swastikas into the ether. It was these men who had supplied Goebbels with the hollow phrases which he used to declare total war. And now these latter-day Leonidases and Nibelungs, who were feted as such in Berlin, handed their pistols over to the first 'Bolshevik subhuman' who stepped into their bunker and meekly allowed themselves to be led away, actions they themselves had described not so many hours earlier as dishonourable and utterly shameful.

'I am not going to put a bullet in my head for the sake of that swine,' said one general and walked out on to the battlefield where 150,000 German soldiers had been sacrificed for that swine, Adolf Hitler. More than 90,000 now dragged themselves with their last ounce of strength – half-starved and riddled with every possible infectious disease – into captivity. But the Red Army had no spare provisions, no shelters and no hospitals in which to bring them back to health. Less than 6,000 of these prisoners were to see their fatherland again.

When von Manstein, the famed strategist and the man who had held the key position at the front, was asked who was responsible for this turn of events, he quoted Hitler's declaration of 6 February 1943: 'I myself bear full responsibility for Stalingrad.' And obviously grateful for this exoneration, he even called this glibly cynical pronouncement 'decent and soldier-like'. It never occurred to him to make the only possible retort: 'Then take the consequences, Herr Hitler, and step down.' Was that too much to expect of a military leader who, day after day, had ordered a hero's death for thousands of soldiers? How much gallantry and the courage of his convictions can one really ask of a field marshal without being thought impertinent? Naturally, when generals look upon themselves as nothing more than an instrument for the transmission of orders, when they no longer accept the responsibilities befitting their status, then indeed Hitler can be said to have borne sole responsibility for everything.

'I suppose you want to kill him,' von Manstein said indignantly a few months later, in the summer of 1943, when a delegate of the conspirators spoke of a long overdue 'reorganization' of the High Command. 'Like a mad dog,' the man replied. Von Manstein would have none of it. It would ruin the army, he declared. But who, in fact, had led the men at Stalingrad and the millions before Moscow to their ruin? Who would eventually usher in the ruination of the entire *Wehrmacht* and of all Germany?

What other justification could the sacrifice of the troops at Stalingrad possibly have had than to use the breathing space it afforded the German Army in the East to put an end to the whole sorry business while there was yet time? To sweep away the man who had led Germany so murderously astray and, in one great act of self-purification before the whole world, save at least a morsel of German honour by calling a halt there and then to the continuous butchery at the front and in the concentration camps, instead of waiting for the victorious Allies to do so on Germany's behalf.

Von Manstein did not have the conspirators' delegate arrested, or hand him over to Hitler's courts. He bowed curtly and declared: 'I am of course at the service of any legal government as Chief of the General Staff.'

Hitler's generals were available to serve once again after the war, in the East and in the West, like tradesmen whose services are retained by whoever may be in control. They built today's *Bundeswehr* and helped to train its officers and generals. Will these, too, be available to serve should some strategic or tactical necessity demand, at a few touches of a button, that a hundred or more Stalingrads be created in Europe?

Civilian Suffering

No one knows exactly how many civilians succumbed to hunger, acts of war and the foul deeds of the murder squads during the Russian campaign in tens of thousands of villages and in the battle-scarred cities of Minsk, Smolensk, Kiev, Odessa, Kharkov, Rostov and Stalingrad. Let us look at the fate of all these millions by taking just one example, Leningrad.

On 30 August 1941, the Germans cut the last railway link to Leningrad south of Lake Ladoga. Thus began the siege of a city with three and a half million inhabitants, a siege that was to last for 882 days. There was just one small loophole to the outside world, across the water or ice of Lake Ladoga between the River Neva near Schlüsselburg and Osinovets, a holiday resort on the lake.

The Soviet government and the Stavka (the Soviet High Command) had almost no preparation for the evacuation, supply or defence of the city, and what little stores of food there were were destroyed by German artillery. Three and a half million people faced the void. Should the city capitulate?

That question was answered by Hitler in his own particular way with a directive following a proposal by General Warlimont for the blockade of Leningrad. It went as follows: 'The Führer has decided to have the city of St Petersburg [Leningrad] wiped off the face of the earth . . . The intention is to close in on the city and to raze it to the ground with artillery and continuous air attacks. Should this lead to an offer of capitulation by the city, that offer will be turned down. The OKW [*Wehrmacht* High Command] is aware of the wish of the German Navy to preserve the docks, the port and the naval installations. That wish cannot however be granted.' In the event, Leningrad offered no capitulation. That was out of the question for Stalin, for Zhdanov, the Communist Party Secretary in the city, and probably for most of the population as well. Between Stalin and Hitler they had, in any case, no option other than to struggle, to starve and to die. In the winter of 1941 one third of the population perished of hunger, over and above those killed by shells and bombs. Imagine all the inhabitants of Birmingham, England, being starved to death in just a few weeks – fifteen times as many people as were killed outright at Hiroshima. And the citizens of Leningrad might well have envied those of Hiroshima their sudden death which came to them like a bolt from the blue.

Soviet writers who survived the siege of Leningrad have recorded the ghastly tragedy for us. But none of their works could be published in its original form at the time – only 'cleaned up' versions were allowed to come out, versions in which there were only heroes, no failures among the leaders, no rogues, no cannibals, no desperadoes, not even half the number of victims. Leningrad was not allowed to remember the full extent of its martyrdom, lest the grandchildren of the survivors came to wonder one day who made it possible in the first place for the Germans to starve their city to death. But does this macabre epilogue of the tragedy of Leningrad really provide the Germans with an alibi?

Treason Behind Barbed Wire

In the course of a badly planned and badly led attempt to relieve Leningrad in the spring of 1942, the Soviet Second Shock Army was surrounded by the Germans near Volkhov. Stalin sent a capable general, Andrei Vlasov, into the pocket to extricate them. Some tens of thousands of Soviet soldiers managed to break through to their own lines, but Vlasov himself was captured by the Germans in July 1942.

By then many a German officer had begun to grasp that the 'silent' liquidation of the Slav masses by the starvation of millions of Soviet prisoners of war was – to quote Talleyrand – worse than a crime, it was rank stupidity. Hundreds of thousands of these prisoners would have been quite prepared to make common cause with the Germans against Stalin if they had been promised just one thing: a free Russia, a free Ukraine or a free Georgia. But it was precisely for these aims that the war was *not* being fought, and it was of course a grotesque illusion to believe that Hitler's war of destruction and pillage could be somehow transformed, against his will and behind his back, into a war of liberation for the people of the Soviet Union.

Paradoxically, it was the very men who served Hitler and his war objectives with the greatest reluctance who succumbed to that illusion. They argued that once the Bolsheviks had been beaten it would be the turn of the Nazi criminals. And they believed that they could thwart Hitler by saving the greatest possible number of Soviet prisoners from the camps. These would be formed into volunteer units who would be used at first to help vanquish the Bolsheviks, and who would return to lands that, once Hitler had been toppled in Germany, would have been rid of the double scourge of Stalin and Hitler. The man who was to become the figurehead of this utterly unrealistic and illusionary policy was General Vlasov, who had by then had quite enough of Stalin's catastrophic policies and strategy. In December 1942 he allowed himself to be persuaded in Berlin – when he was allegedly in Smolensk – to set up a 'Committee for the Liberation of the Peoples of Russia' with the objective of creating a Russian Freedom Army. That Committee called upon the Red Army and Soviet civilians, through broadcasts and leaflets, to rise up against Stalin. But the German leaflets bearing Vlasov's signature were sent raining down on the Red Army just as the Soviet Union was celebrating its spectacular victory at Stalingrad. Which Red Army soldier would, at that moment, have wanted to exchange a triumphant Stalin for a defeated Hitler? True, the Germans managed to put together a few Russian units on their side of the front, but they were predominantly made up of minorities traditionally oppressed by the Russians – Georgians, Azerbaijanis, Armenians, Caucasians and Turkestanis. Many of these men were not allowed to fight for the 'liberation' of their homelands on the Eastern Front, but were frequently made to risk their necks for Hitler elsewhere. For though these 'volunteers' had been rescued from Hitler's hunger camps, they were made to pay for it. At the end of the war, the Allies shamefully handed them back to the Soviet Union, where they ended up in front of Stalin's execution squads or in the Gulag camps. Here they could have met the one million of the five million Soviet prisoners of war who had survived the war and who, after their repatriation, had also been banished to the Gulag Archipelago as traitors and deserters. As with Leningrad, the Soviet government did not want its subjects reminded of the terrible fate of their prisoners of war; to this day the Soviet people have not been told that almost four million of their sons perished in German captivity. Least of all must they be reminded that the omniscient and omnipotent Soviet leadership was unable to prevent the Germans from taking five million Soviet soldiers prisoner in the first place.

In purely ideological respects the Soviet Union looked upon 'ordinary enemy combatants', once they had been captured and disarmed, as potential allies who had only gone to war out of blindness or under coercion and who had to be politically re-educated. Theirs was unquestionably a far more humane attitude than that of the Nazis. But it was only a theory.

The practice on the Eastern Front was quite different. In 1941 the *Wehrmacht* posted 46,000 men missing. No one knows how many of them were taken prisoner. Quite apart from the numerous well-documented murders of German prisoners of war, many of which could have been blamed on burning resentment of the treacherous attack by the German *Wehrmacht* and the terrible losses it had brought in its wake, the quartering and provisioning of the prisoners during transportation and in the camps were so wretched, and the production targets they were set so hard, that prisoners were unlikely to survive for long. The rations allocated on paper would have been adequate had they actually reached the prisoners, but because of the vast dislocation caused by the German onslaught and the catastrophic food situation of the population at large – the *Wehrmacht* had captured an area which had formerly produced some 50 per cent of Soviet food supplies, in any case deficient – that never happened. Soviet citizens, too, were starving and not in Leningrad alone. The whole country was going hungry and every Soviet citizen had to fight for bare survival. In this struggle for existence the German prisoner of war came off worst – few Soviet citizens had any scruples about filching his bread, for was he not the source of all their latest, extreme privation?

Even so, as late as November 1941, the Soviet government had issued a diplomatic note protesting against the treatment of their prisoners of war by the Germans and proposing an agreement on the treatment of prisoners on both sides. But Hitler brushed this aside. As far as he was concerned, German prisoners in the Soviet Union were few and far between, and those few that the Red Army had laid their hands on would have to look after themselves. The German leadership was not interested. As for Soviet prisoners of war, the more of them that died, the better.

The Russians largely entrusted the political re-education of German prisoners to German communist emigrants whom they appointed 'polit-instructors' under the supervision of Soviet political officers. These men, too, did not entertain particularly warm feelings for their fellow country-men, who had fought so staunchly for Hitler. Moreover, they found themselves caught between the devil and the deep blue sea. Since they were Germans, the Soviet security apparatus looked upon them as potential Fascists and enemies of the Soviet Union. More than half of their comrades had, during the Soviet purges in the thirties, disappeared into Soviet camps and been shot. On the other hand, their political re-education efforts were bound to fail, if only because although every-thing they said about Hitler and Hitlerism may have been accurate and true, they were not allowed to breathe one word of truth in answer to the oft-repeated questions about conditions in the Soviet Union and the cause of Soviet defeats. That would have been tantamount to criticizing Stalinism and would have meant certain death.

Their Marxist appeals to the pacifist and internationalist ideals of the working-class, to solidarity in the fight against Hitler – that 'watchdog of monopoly capitalism', as they simplistically called him – rebounded as so much empty verbiage from the firm Nazi convictions of most of the prisoners. Their references to German war crimes were dismissed as nothing but atrocity-mongering, or else compared to Bolshevik crimes and so played down or even justified, and their conviction that Nazi Germany would lose the war was greeted with derision. Most German prisoners of war believed that they were on the point of being liberated by the victorious *Wehrmacht*.

The 'politinstructors' were set a certain quota of conversions which they had to fulfil or be accused of ideological weakness. That is why they so often resorted to the carrot-and-stick method, to bribery with offers of remunerative posts in the camp on the one hand, and to threats of incarceration, accusations of Fascist incitement and backbreaking labour on the other. As a result, they discredited the small minority of honest anti-Fascists, whom no one could any longer distinguish from the 'kash-ists' – those who had sold their convictions for a spoonful of *kasha*, porridge.

The situation in the camps remained much the same until the Stalingrad winter. The Soviet leadership had meanwhile realized that their original hopes for an effective resistance by the German working-class, let alone for a mass uprising in Germany, had been entirely misplaced. Hence even before the German Sixth Army was encircled near Stalingrad, Stalin made an appeal to the old allies of the Red Army, to those *Wehrmacht* generals who could still recall the close collaboration of the two forces in the twenties. In his address to the Supreme Soviet on 6 November 1942, he said, *inter alia*: 'Our aim is not the destruction of Germany, but we can and must destroy the Hitler state. We have no wish to destroy all organized military forces in Germany, for every educated person knows that . . . is impossible and, from the victor's viewpoint, inexpedient. But we can and must smash the Hitler Army.'

What else could these words have been other than a barely disguised appeal to the leaders of the *Wehrmacht* to overthrow Hitler, to end the war, thus saving both countries from further massacres and opening the way to a new partnership? Of the 90,000 German prisoners taken at Stalingrad, more than 90 per cent were dead within a few weeks. In the physical state in which they were caught – pitifully undernourished and riddled with infectious disease – and in the prevailing conditions, the Soviets would have had to be true Samaritans to save them. In the event, they saw very little reason for such Christian neighbourly love. Even so, twenty-one generals and more than 2,000 officers survived, and it was these men that the Soviet leaders now tried desperately to win over as allies.

Those who lived through the catastrophe of Stalingrad had to be more than a little slow-witted not to wonder whether Germany under Hitler was on the right road, whether the 'Führer' really was the brilliant statesman and general he had appeared to be in 1940 and even as late as August 1941. Opponents of Hitler who came out of Stalingrad alive were few and far between, and the term is used here to refer only to those who had realized even before Stalingrad that Hitler was a criminal, not just because he had lost the war but also because, if given his way, he would destroy his people and their country. However, under the impact of defeat, many Germans were beginning to have doubts about the blessings of National Socialism, doubts they had repressed in the intoxication of Hitler's victories.

Paradoxically, through captivity the prisoners regained a degree of freedom they had not enjoyed for a long time. They were able at last to discuss National Socialism frankly, without the threat of a court martial or the Gestapo hanging over them. Soviet re-education efforts undoubtedly fuelled these discussions considerably, and accelerated the process of rethinking that now set in. Moreover, in view of the military position and the millions of murders committed by the Nazis, to which it was impossible any longer to turn a blind eye, there was no need for the Soviets to resort to some fiendish form of brain-washing for a growing number of prisoners to realize that Hitlerism meant the ruination of Germany.

It was against that background that the Soviets, through communist emigrants in Moscow, offered the captives a chance to set up their own 'National Committee for a Free Germany' which would exhort the German people and the *Wehrmacht* to 'call a halt now while there is still time'.

The committee was founded in Moscow in July 1943. In its manifesto, drafted after heated discussions between the leaders of the German emigrants and a few German officers, the Communists – on a nod from the Soviets – dropped all their old revolutionary demands and appeals to the class struggle. Unlike the appeals of the Vlasov Committee, those of the Free Germany Committee were based on a sober and truthful analysis of the military situation. No external enemy had ever caused Germany as much misery as Hitler, they pointed out. The war was lost, yet no one would make peace with Hitler or even negotiate with him. The only road to peace was through his overthrow. A new German government would have to march the *Wehrmacht* back to the borders of the Reich, renounce all conquests, put an end to Nazi crimes and restore the constitutional state. Only then could the German people hope to recover the right to determine their own future and to be listened to by the world. No promises were made. On the contrary, it was stated with brutal sobriety what Germany could expect if Hitler were removed, not by the Germans themselves but by the Allies: the end of national independence and the break-up of the Fatherland.

The aims and arguments of the Free Germany Committee were thus identical with those of the opposition inside Germany. The only question was what the Soviets hoped to gain from making common cause with men who still put Germany first. If the object was to 'bolshevize' Germany, then Hitler should have been given enough leeway to drag down with him all those who were still capable of halting the advance of Bolshevism into Central Europe. A premature overthrow of Hitler by the Germans themselves could not serve this purpose. It would, however, save other countries an untold number of victims and create conditions for future political collaboration. Seen in that light, the Soviet people and the Germans did indeed have a common interest in an anti-Hitler coup. The Soviet authorities, moreover, may also have been afraid that, given the hopeless situation of Hitler's Germany, such a coup was on the cards in any event but with a purely Western bias. Did they therefore just wish to use the Free Germany Committee as a line to Berlin in case the call should be answered not by Hitler and Ribbentrop, but by such men as Beck, Schulenberg or Hassel, who were working to overthrow Hitler? But even that need not have harmed the German opposition, but might, on the contrary, have extended its scope for negotiation. In any case it does not take too much imagination to realize how much better and more honourably Germany would have emerged from the end of the war had the *Wehrmacht* produced the responsible leaders appealed for by the Free Germany Committee to end the war in 1943 or even in July 1944.

Alas, these appeals faded away over the Russian battlefields much as Vlasov's had done. The belated anti-Hitler conspiracy came to nothing, and Soviet hopes in the Committee crumbled away. It was then that they decided to transform that part of Germany allocated to them as a zone of occupation after Germany's total defeat, into one of their satellites.

General von Seydlitz, who had wanted to act against Hitler at Stalingrad and who, in keeping with that stand, had placed himself at the disposal of the Free Germany Committee when he was a prisoner of war, was sentenced to death and not by Hitler alone. A Soviet court followed suit in 1950. Later he was 'pardoned' and his sentence commuted to twenty-five years' imprisonment. He was allowed to return to Germany in 1955 after five years of solitary confinement. There a court ruled that he had acted honourably, but that he could not become a general of the *Bundeswehr* – even had he been younger. That honour was reserved for his enemies in Soviet captivity, men who had wanted him to be lifted out by paratroopers and who had even given serious consideration to plans to murder him and his comrades.

In the end some 3,500,000 German soldiers finished up in Russian hands. Of these, 1,200,000 did not survive, about the same number as the Russians who had starved to death in Leningrad. Many did not die until the winter of 1946/7, when, as the Soviet Union was stricken with drought and suffered widespread starvation once more, the Allies discontinued their food supplies.

Forty Years On

Thanks to the complaisance of the German generals, Hitler was granted his Wagnerian dream of destruction in the bunker beneath his old Chancellery, in blazing Berlin. His death brought to an end the unnatural alliance he had forged with himself, and in the process the remains of the German Reich were also torn asunder. Ever since, the victorious Allies of old have confronted each other in Germany face to face. Nowadays no such monsters as Stalin and Hitler are needed to unleash a new apocalypse. It will be enough for a tiny microchip in a computer to go mad, and for someone to feel there is no alternative but to press the button and obliterate hundreds of cities. In 1914, too, the world's statesmen thought only of deterrence as they mobilized, until such time as they had no alternative but 'forward flight'. Faith in nuclear missiles as peacemakers is no whit more realistic or reasonable now than the arms race then. And if the arming of one side leads automatically to the rearming of the other we are surely allowed to ask whether the converse might not also apply: that disarmament invites disarmament.

It is unfortunately true that Stalin's heirs still rule the Soviet Union. But does fear of them not conceal a proper share of the bad conscience about the 30 million victims of the German onslaught against their homeland? To most Germans the war against Russia is old history. In reality it is part and parcel of their here and now, since its consequences are still Germany's greatest problem. For that reason, we should remember what it was really like.

Grasbrunn
December 1983

Heinrich, Graf von Einsiedel

48

The Onslaught

Generalgouvernement
für die besetzten polnischen Gebiete
.
Grenze
14 m.

Grenze

1   Soviet-occupied Poland began 14 metres beyond this frontier sign on the River Granitsa. German-held ~~P~~oland, the so-called Government General, comprised the lowlands on either side of the Upper and ~~Ce~~ntral Vistula down to the south of Warsaw; in the East it extended to the River Bug and in the South to ~~th~~e summits of the Carpathians

2

2.   Men from a German Sixth Army infantry unit attending divine service in the field before going into battle. They had not been told what their objectives were: a drive from the south of the Government General towards Kiev and the Dnieper

3.   German soldiers reporting to their marshalling areas on bicycles. The regrouping of German units in the deployment area began as early as February–March 1941

4.   German troops overran the border fortifications very quickly. East of Krystynopol, 2 kilometres beyond the frontier, they came within range of the concrete border bunkers. The ensuing battles lasted two days before the Soviet troops retreated. Both sides recorded their first casualties

3

5

5–8.   By 27 June 1941, the German Sixth Army had reached the Radzikhov–Lopatin–Lezhniov–Snurdare Line. Tanks and artillery were used by the defending forces in an attempt to halt the attack. The pictures show shot-up tanks and the results of artillery in action at Radzikhov–Kholoyov

6

9. In many Ukrainian villages German soldiers were welcomed as liberators from Stalinist oppression. On 14 July 1941, Stalin called on the people of the USSR to engage in partisan warfare, but many Ukrainians preferred to serve as partisans against their own compatriots

10. Dead horses on the road to Vitkovnovy

11. After the first major German losses, divisional cemeteries were set up behind the front lines. Here the dead were brought for burial

12.   As always in war, children were the innocent victims: this picture shows war orphans being picked up by the *Wehrmacht*

13.   A German dispatch rider ferrying a Soviet prisoner of war on the pillion of his motor cycle to an assembly point behind the lines. During the first few weeks of the war the Germans advanced so quickly that they captured many thousands of Red Army soldiers

14.   Prisoners of war from the Asiatic republics of the Soviet Union: Uzbeks, Tadzhiks, and many others. Since only a few of them spoke Russian, it was almost impossible to communicate with them

15.   Local inhabitants trying to flee from the battle zone

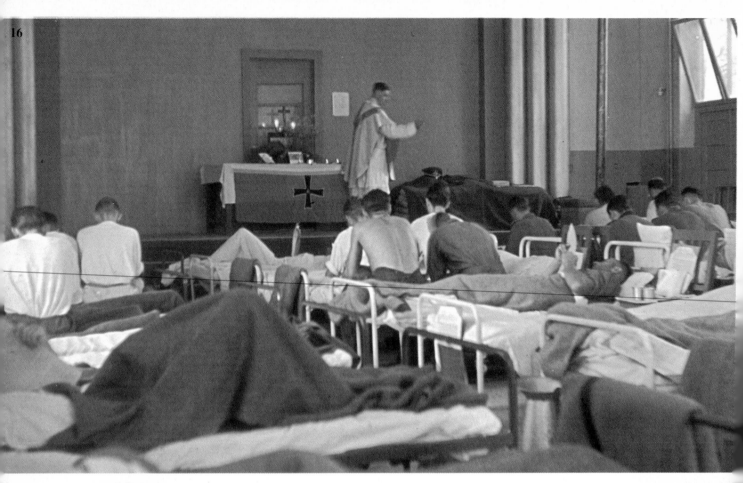

18

16.   Services were held regularly in hospitals behind the lines for both Lutherans and Catholics

17.   Despite the heavy fighting, services in the field continued to be attended by large numbers of German soldiers

18.   There was little time to bury the dead. On the verge of the main street in Cherkassy, captured by the Germans eight weeks after the invasion, two soldiers have been buried in hastily dug graves, marked by sunflowers. The violent resistance led to heavy losses on both sides

19.   On 24 October 1941 German troops occupied Kharkov, then the capital of the Ukraine. The tall blocks of flats on Red Square showed little sign of damage despite the fierce battles that had raged before the fall of the city. At about that time, it became known that the Führer was planning a drive on Stalingra in the direction of the Caucasus

20. Winter set in at the beginning of November 1941 and turned out to be one of the coldest in Eastern Europe this century. The 'muddy season' caused by alternating snowfalls and rainstorms immobilized attackers and defenders alike. Ice floes on the Dnieper smashed the temporary bridges built by the Germans

21. Even during the summer, heavy rains in this region posed grave problems for the motorized units. So-called *Hiwis*, volunteers from prisoner-of-war camps, were assigned to help the transport units. Their provisions were much better than in the camps

22. From a German Army communiqué of 10 September 1941: 'Weather cold and dull, with occasional torrential rain. Roads still impassable.' A jeep has slid off a track, the former main road near Cherkassy, into a bomb crater

23 and 25. Many German soldiers had to try and survive the icy Russian winter in their summer uniforms

24. On 14 November 1941, the first frosts set in and at Kharkov the thermometer read minus 22°C. The German soldiers' equipment was wholly inadequate: the few snow tunics they had been issued with were purely for camouflage and offered no protection against the freezing cold

26.   On 4 January 1942, the Sixth
Army meteorologist recorded a
temperature of 42°C below zero.
Severe frost and deep snowdrifts
badly hampered the German supply
lines. Hitler's vaunted *blitzkrieg* had
ground to a halt. Not even the most
up-to-date technology could cope
with the unusual weather conditions.
As a result, horses came into their
own once again, and had to be
requisitioned throughout the Reich.
They were not enough, however, to
effect any improvement in the
terrible transport conditions

27.   The severe winter was followed by even more 'muddy seasons' before the weather began to get warmer and the frosts were definitely over. The depleted German troops were quickly reinforced with units from Germany and from occupied Western Europe, in order that fighting could be resumed

Advance on the Ukraine

At the request of the local population, a church still standing in Novoya Vodolaga is reopened. The ~~st~~, who had been afraid of persecution under Soviet rule and had gone into hiding as a worker on a ~~khoz~~ (collective farm), now allows himself to be photographed in his vestments. Yet idyllic dreams of ~~ration~~ were short-lived. Soon afterwards the Ukrainian people were to suffer cruelly at the hands of the ~~and~~ *Wehrmacht* special commandos

29

30

31

32

29–31.   Soldiers on a train journey to the front, trying to amuse themselves as best they can – at the halts there were even opportunities for relaxing with a book. Only those in the orderly rooms, and members of Propaganda Companies (known as PK-reporters for short) were issued with typewriters. These men still seem largely untouched by the horrors of war

32.   Once at their destination, they pitched their tents and awaited further orders. A period of uncertainty began

33.   A main road in Kharkov in the spring of 1942. Thousands of wheels, horses' hooves and marching boots have turned the road into a river of mud. These extremely arduous conditions were to continue until the heavy rainfall came to an end in the summer

34

34. Towards the middle of May, in the course of the spring offensive, Soviet units near Kharkov managed to breach the German lines in several places. German relief units were frequently set down before reaching the front line. These are units of the Bodensee Division near Karavanskoye, brought up to strengthen the defences. The men sink exhausted to the ground during a brief pause in their forced march to the front

35 and 36. Only a small section of the German army was motorized, including the dispatch riders who carried intelligence and orders to the widely scattered command posts. Progress on the muddy roads was often a matter of co-operation

37–39. In the steppes east of the Ukraine there were no road signs and few landmarks by which the Germans could take their bearings. Good maps were few and far between. As a result German patrols and dispatch riders had to ask their way of women and old men working in the fields. The poor planning and the consequent foundering of the German troops in the vastnesses of the unchartered territory are reflected in these typical everyday scenes

39

40.   Outside Stalino, motorized units await orders for their continued advance

41 and 42.   The town was captured on 21 October 1941: it was badly damaged in the fighting. It was one of the last large towns to be taken on the German march to the East

43.   PK reporters were largely responsible for the picture of the war formed by the German people at home. Cameras were attended to and reports put together behind the lines

44.   Members of a Propaganda Company in their car. Such transport not only provided greater mobility but often enabled reporters to be on the spot for a good story

45.   At the time, horses were the troops' best friends, but they were driven to the limits of their endurance. When severely wounded they were taken to the horse-butcher who turned their carcasses into extra rations

47

46. The battles near Kharkov and along the Don led to the complete destruction of many small villages

47. Thousands of Red Army men were taken prisoner. Because of the difficult German supply situation and as a result of the various prohibitions and regulations issued by the military and political authorities, the care of Soviet prisoners of war was extraordinarily bad. In particular, the civilian population was not allowed to supply them with food. Many starved to death, were shot during transportation, or died of exhaustion or from such diseases as typhus. In countless prisoner-of-war camps, no kind of shelter was provided for the inmates, so that thousands lingered in the open, braving rain and snow. During the autumn of 1941, up to 2,500 Soviet prisoners died each day in the Ukrainian camps

50

48–50.   In the spring of 1942 there were many sudden changes in the weather in the Kharkov district. In a situatin report for 'Führer HQ' on 3 May 1942, General Franz Halder let it be known that Sixth Army transporters could only negotiate roads with the help of horse-drawn vehicles. Even tanks had great difficulty in advancing

51 and 52.   Life and death are but moments apart. These four men from a South German infantry patrol have found a sheltered corner to rest for a few minutes during their strenuous advance, using it to have a meal and read their letters. The army postal service reached these widely dispersed and fast moving patrols only rarely, so that news from home was usually several weeks old

53.   A short time later, a Soviet sub-machine-gun has mowed the men down. Four human lives are wiped out. The *Wehrmacht* communiqué for that day: 'No special engagements'

54.   A line of crosses, 2,000 kilometres from home: German losses kept mounting. From 22 June 1941 to 20 March 1942, the Eastern Front claimed 796,516 wounded, 224,659 killed and 50,941 missing. Of the 750 men in a company, often no more than twenty to thirty were left. Local skirmishes alone took a tremendous toll. These losses could no longer be made good

55–57. Once the Germans had reached the Kalmuck steppe in a fresh summer offensive in 1942, aircraft on either side ceased to play a decisive role except on rare occasions. Here there were neither river crossings nor bunkers over which aircraft could be usefully deployed on bombing raids. German and Soviet planes shot down or forced to make emergency landings were very carefully gone over by the men. Picture 56 shows a German *Fieseler Storch* (Stork), a popular single-engine monoplane used for liaison and general utility work, after a crash-landing

58.   Time and again, German troops in the steppe passed huge columns of Soviet soldiers being marched into captivity. They had all fought in battles that achieved sad notoriety. One hundred and three thousand Red Army men were captured at Uman early in August 1941, and at the end of September 1941 a further 665,000 were captured at Kiev. These prisoners, most of them totally

exhausted, were forced to march distances of up to 500 kilometres as the crow flies to camps in occupied Poland or in East Prussia, covering up to 40 kilometres a day. About 3.3 million of a total of 5.7 million Soviet prisoners of war died in German captivity during the Second World War

59–60.   Pause outside Kalach: the soldiers rest on one arm, unable to lie flat because of their heavy packs. They were not allowed to take these off because they had to be ready to move on at a moment's notice. The rider stays on his horse, probably because he was too tired to dismount and remount without help. In such situations it was a great boon to belong to a motorized unit

59

60

61. A German machine-gunner firing at an enemy patrol

62. The direct attack on Stalingrad began on 13 September 1942. By the end of August 1942 a German patrol had crossed the River Oskol. Shortly after this photograph was taken, a Soviet gun destroyed the rest of the bridge. The photographer took the picture from under cover just a few yards from the Soviet line of defence

63

63.   The flat terrain made it possible to see enemy action from a long way away, hence the relaxed attitudes of these men watching the impact of an exploding shell. Despite the catastrophic results of his winter campaign of 1941–2, Hitler planned an even fiercer onslaught, especially in the Caucasus. Germa panzer spearheads continued to drive wedges to the East and South

64.   In July 1942 the *Wehrmacht* reached the foothills of the Kalmuck steppe, west of the Volga. This plain runs west of the Lower Volga down to the Kuma lowlands

65.   The almost treeless plain is cut in places by deeply-eroded valleys. Here prisoners were herded together, a safe watch being kept on them from the ridges. At other times these valleys offered good cover to attackers and defenders alike

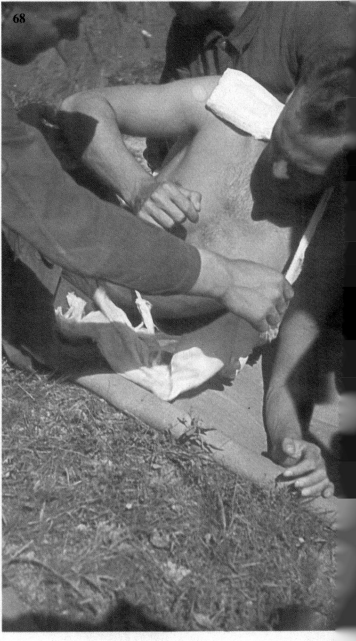

66.   Soviet infantry advancing over open terrain. The snapshot conveys the sense of surprise and threat the photographer must have felt. The haste with which he pulled out his camera is reflected in this slightly blurred picture

67 and 68.   A wounded German infantryman being carried out of the fighting lines, and a little while later being given an emergency dressing. With few exceptions, the medical care of the German troops was good, though there were supply problems due to the large distances involved. Not every wounded soldier was taken to hospital; doctors at the main field dressing station decided whether casualties were to be treated on the spot or sent to a hospital in the rear. Distances to the nearest hospital could be anything from 100 to 700 kilometres

69.   A quick memento taken before the vast Ukrainian sunflower fields were left behind – an idyllic break in the horrors of war

70–73. At first, contacts between German soldiers and the local population were easy-going. However, because of the methods of the Nazi administration, they very quickly became oppressive. Those local inhabitants still capable of doing work were transported to forced labour in the Reich, while the special commandos and 'Action Groups' abducted countless others and murdered them

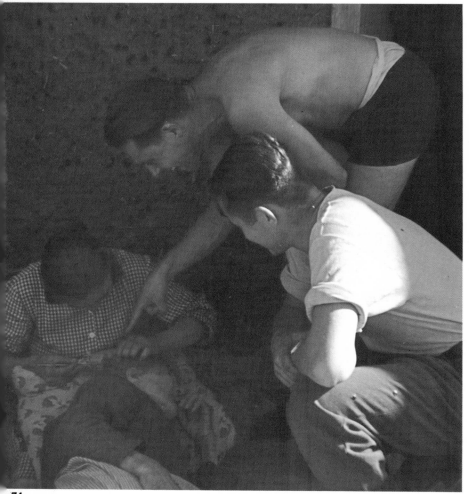

73

74–76. These women from Poltava in their national costume had probably been left without news of their husbands and sons for weeks. Their friendliness towards the Germans was no doubt dictated by fears for their own fate. Their uncertainty, deepened by communication problems, is easily detected here, despite appearances to the contrary

74

76

photo on right side

77. After the occupation of the Ukraine, the *Wehrmacht* counted and registered the population. This particular census is near Stalino. This registration served later, among other things, to single out for seizure all those fit for work.

In the Ukraine, a considerable proportion of the population was Jewish. Jews were often murdered on the spot by special commandos; the others were transported to concentration camps. A decree by Hitler of December 1941 authorized the special commandos to 'punish the population for offences against the Reich or the occupying power with the death penalty'. Executions were frequently carried out without any legal preliminaries. This and following decrees and ordinances were aimed at all acts construed as 'endangering the security of the occupying power', which were then punished without mercy

78–80. Despite fierce resistance here and there from the Red Army, the German Sixth Army continued its brisk advance. Many of the widely dispersed units were strengthened with *Hiwi* reinforcements. The Sixth Army communiqué of 17 July 1942 states laconically: 'Our units have gained ground in the East according to plan'. Where there were no roads, German vehicles rolled wide tracks through the countryside. The weather here was fine and hot. One of the photographers noted: 'We have no more maps and can only follow the compass needle to the East . . .!'

80

81.   General Paulus, Commander
of the Sixth Army, on his way to a
briefing at his quarters in Poltava.
On 1 July 1942 the Sixth Army
launched a fresh offensive. Hitler
had, surprisingly, split Army Group
South into Groups A and B. In the
meantime the Soviet arms industry
had greatly stepped up its output.
The political and military leadership
of the Soviet Union was determined
to halt the drive on the vital supply
line of the Volga at all costs

Summer Offensive 1942

. Secure quarters were few and far between on the road to Stalingrad and did not stretch to commodate the troops. By the time the German units entered a place, most of the houses were either stroyed or occupied by earlier arrivals, so that the soldiers were forced to camp out in the open nearly the time

83–88.   Rivers posed no obstacle to either side. Thus a Sixth Army communiqué reported on 23 July 1942 that, according to aerial observation and enemy reports, a Soviet division and some 200 enemy tanks had landed at Kalach, 75 kilometres from Stalingrad. That division had orders to halt the German advance from the West at the Liska, and to establish a line of defence between the Don and the Volga. The German Army Command then made great efforts to bring up tanks and reinforcements for its own front. To that end, sturdy bridges and ferries were constructed on reaches of the river behind the front

86

87

88

89 and 90.   On 15 August 1942, the German Sixth Army advanced on the great north-east loop of the Don, north of Kalach, and used the fearful German rocket launchers to devastating effect

91.   One of the photographers noted nevertheless: 'When we crossed the Don on 17 August, we suffered the heaviest losses of the whole Russian campaign. First Company lost twenty-eight men, Second Company lost twenty men and Third Company twenty-one men.' A constant stream of casualties poured into the main field dressing station. Our eye-witness continued: 'Our doctors and medical orderlies often have to work for up to 36 hours at a stretch to try and "patch up" the wounded so that they can at least be taken to the rear by ambulance plane or truck'

92 and 93.   A bridgehead right at the front. Tanks being taken across the Don over improvised or repaired bridges at Kalach

94.   Worn out and ruined equipment litters the river bank. The German advance continued to the 'blocking position' north of Stalingrad

95.   In the southern sector of the Stalingrad front, the Red Army suffered heavy losses. 'South of Stalingrad, the enemy has brought up reinforcements and is putting up fierce resistance' (Sixth Army communiqué). The two German soldiers cheerfully having their photograph taken in front of the cynical epitaph on a Soviet soldiers' burial place (the sign means 'Russians' Hard Luck Villa'), seem to have no inkling of the appalling end that probably lay in store for them

96.   Local people waiting helplessly and apathetically for the fighting to stop in their area

97–99. Using whatever cover the village houses afford them, Red Army soldiers try to hold up the German advance. During the fighting, it was no longer possible to consider the few civilians left living in the bullet-ridden houses

100.   According to an official communiqué of 18 August 1942, 'the Sixth Army has suffered few losses during the past few days'. This respite was due to a lull in the German attack which the communiqué failed to mention. Time and again, German soldiers passed mile-long lines of Soviet prisoners of war. From the late autumn of 1942, most Red Army prisoners were packed off for labour service in the Reich where the failure of Hitler's plan for quick victory had caused an acute labour shortage in the armaments industry. At that juncture, all Nazi sensibilities on making use of the services of 'sub-humans' were forgotten. By the end of October 1942, Hitler personally sanctioned the 'deployment' of prisoners in German industry

101. Hitler was unswerving in his opinion that the enemy had been beaten, a view many German soldiers at the front now no longer shared. Their contact with the civilian population had shown them that the Soviet citizen differed radically from the 'Bolshevik subhuman' of Nazi propaganda

102

103

104

102–108.   Soviet infantry, in a hopelessly exposed position on a farm, try vainly to halt the attacking Germans by putting them under fire. Their resistance is broken with a few bursts of German artillery fire. Such episodes drove home to the German soldiers how fierce the Red Army's continuing spirit of resistance was, a state of affairs in stark contrast to that generally conveyed in communiqués from Führer HQ

105

106

107

108

09–112. '. . . According to intelligence reports, very strong panzer concentrations of US origin have entered the Stalingrad sector.' This claim in the Sixth Army communiqué of 16 August 1942 was soon to be corroborated, for when the Red Army, using 150 tanks, tried to counterattack a short time later and was repulsed with heavy losses on both sides, the German troops in this sector had their first glimpse of US markings on an enemy tank

113 and 115. :Communiqué of 23 August 1942: ¡Fourth Panzer Army of Army Group B has made little progress for lack of fuel and ammunition.' Similar shortages made themselves felt throughout the Sixth Army. The only solution was to capture Soviet fuel supplies. Smashed and burned-out vehicles are left as worthless scrap or dragged away at night behind their own lines by Soviet soldiers

114. A Soviet mine may look harmless but will explode at the slightest touch

116

117

116. Self-propelled Red Army rocket launchers which the Germans soon nicknamed 'Stalin Organs'

117. When tanks were hit they usually burnt out completely, often incinerating their crews

118. The German drive on Stalingrad ground to a halt as fewer and fewer anti-tank weapons became available. The resulting lulls in the fighting were used by overtired soldiers to snatch brief naps. At about this time, the popular singer Wilhelm Strienz used to sing requests on German radio programmes for the troops. One of his songs had the line: 'Soldiers now crave sleep not dreams. . .'

118

119.   North of Stalingrad, between the Don and the Volga, German troops established a 150-kilometre long blocking position against attacks from the north. It was essential to maintain radio contact along this lengthy front

120.   The Soviet defenders were ensconced behind concrete bunkers set into the ground

121.   Companies were often reduced to a handful of men; for weeks no more reinforcements had arrived. Every six yards or so there were holes dug in the ground with one or two soldiers 'in occupation'

122

123

122 and 124.   Front-line foxholes: swastika flags served as markers for German aircraft

123.   One of our photographers wearing 'captured' articles of clothing on the blocking position, August 1942. Many German soldiers wore articles of clothing taken from the bodies of fallen Red Army men. Equipment, too, was no longer being replaced. For weeks at a time, no change of clothing was possible.

A situation report to Hitler on 28 August read: 'Colonel General Baron von Richthofen has . . . personally examined the stiuation at Stalingrad and as a result of these observations, and also from consultations with the Commanders of the Fourth Panzer Army and of the Sixth Army, he has established that there is no question of further strong enemy resistance . . . The General's overall impression was that the enemy lacked a unified command . . .'

125.   In one of the many eroded *balkas* (gullies) outside Stalingrad, an army chaplain gives general absolution to an infantry battalion about to attack the city. What lies in store for these men, weighed down by the fear of impending death? The service is intended to calm their nerves and perhaps to offer

them a little solace as well. Only a few would survive the inferno. 'You could count them on the fingers of one hand.'

126. At a time when a Sixth Army communiqué spoke of 'favourable developments in the fighting round Stalingrad', many German companies had been reduced to just a few men

127. One of our photographers reported: 'On 13 October we formed up for battle and on 14 October came the attack on North Stalingrad'

Stalingrad

28.   By the autumn of 1942, Stalingrad had been reduced to a confused and broken jumble of
dwellings, machine shops and factories. The city measured some 10 kilometres wide by 40 kilometres
long, and was crossed at irregular intervals by *balkas*. Had the German *Wehrmacht*, or rather its High
Command, heeded the sign ('Entry to Stalingrad is at risk to life') they themselves had put up,
thousands of German soldiers would have been spared

129.   The northern part of Stalingrad was taken by German troops on 14 October. It did not take long for the city to become a scene of utter desolation

130.   The grain silo in the centre of the city is recognizable in the distance

131.   Houses in north Stalingrad were built for the most part of clay and straw. Fire and shells left only the chimneys standing

132.   Plaster figures of children playing beside the graves of German soldiers in south Stalingrad – a picture that is almost surreal. The further the Germans advanced towards the heart of the city, the greater became the destruction, those walls still standing being used by the soldiers as building material for bunkers.

   The Army communiqué of 16 September 1942 read: 'The southern flank of the Sixth Army has made good progress. On the Führer's orders, the battle for Stalingrad will be placed under the unified command of the Sixth Army . . . Attacks were hampered by sandstorms.'

133.   As early as 2 September 1942,
Hitler had ordered: 'Upon taking
Stalingrad, the entire male
population is to be removed . . .'
The local population attempted to
flee the inferno of the battles.
Women and children tied up what
few possessions they had left, often
into only one bundle, to take away
with them

134.   Despite all the horrors, a few
stayed behind in the ruins of their
houses. Water and food were fast
running out. The washing on the line
is all that is left of house and home

134

135. Sixth Army communiqué of 8 October: 'No particular fighting to report in Stalingrad.' In fact, that is how it often was. German soldiers took refuge in ruined buildings, and the only fighting units left, made up of eight to ten men each, were scattered. They formed the entire 'front', and were bombarded day and night by Soviet guns. The twisted cross in the foreground of the picture seems to symbolize the God-forsaken nature of the place

136 and 137.   Families with small children decided in many cases not to risk leaving the city, because their children were too weak to stand up to long marches. Fear of being caught in the crossfire also persuaded many to hang on in the city's *balkas*

138.   German soldiers could not offer assistance even had they wanted to. They too were desperately short of food

139–142.   Those few inhabitants who stayed behind – at the end of the fighting they numbered barely 1,500 – kept getting between the lines. The extent of the destruction and the strength of these people's will to survive are reflected in these moving pictures

The Sixth Army communiqué of 30 Otober 1942 read: 'The Sixth Army will continue its attack on Stalingrad, first dealing with resistance groups in the south of the city.'

139

140

141

143. The ruins of a housing estate in Stalingrad are reminiscent of the later bombed-out cities in Germany. A German soldier captured at Stalingrad was met by a Soviet officer with the words: 'That's how your Berlin will look one of these days.'

144–146.   The destruction of the city continued unabated. The High Command of Germany Army Group B tried as long as possible to follow orders and to hold parts of Stalingrad and the bank of the Volga. According to the High Command, the city, though devastated, provided better cover in the winter than the bare steppe between the Don and the Volga. By September it had become clear that the Germans would not be able to drive the Red Army out of the city. An increasing number of German wounded had to be flown out by ambulance plane and these men were later to be among the lucky survivors

When Hitler was asked to shorten the Don front in order to release reserves, he refused point blank. On 6 October the Army Group High Command accordingly issued the following order: 'The situation at Stalingrad, the capture of which the Führer has again described as the most important objective of the Army Group, demands the concentration of all available forces. All other objectives must take second place.'

147

148

149

150

147 and 148.   On 15 October 1942, the Germans captured the tractor factory, the brick works and a number of housing settlements in north Stalingrad

149.   Mortars were set up at particularly fiercely contested positions

150.   Soviet soldiers had taken shelter in the building in the background

151.   On 16 October, as one of the
photographers recorded, the
Germans launched an assault on the
'Red Barricade' gun factory. In one
of the works they came across
machines in the vast assembly area
bearing the plates of a German firm
in Göppingen.

    A lull in the fighting in this part of
the city followed, which lasted until
29 October

152.   From a photographer's report: 'Towards the end of the month, we attacked a fuel depot on the Volga. This picture shows the easternmost point of Russia we have reached. In front of us lies the last tract of ground to the Volga, full of craters, hills and bunkers . . .'

A German patrol which had crossed the Volga was wiped out by Soviet soldiers with hand grenades. The date was 16 October 1942

The following black and white photographs by Soviet reporters record the end of the fighting in Stalingrad, the German capitulation and the long march of German soldiers into captivity

153. A Soviet patrol on Mamaev
Hill in the centre of Stalingrad

154. Red Army men surrounding
the 'Red October' steel plant

155 and 157.   Soviet soldiers of the 62nd Army during house to house fighting in Stalingrad

156.   Red Army men firing from a trench

158.   Stalingrad is cloaked in flames and clouds of smoke

157

158

159

159. A department store in Stalingrad whose basement had been used as a command post by Field Marshal Paulus, Commander in Chief of the German Sixth Army. The swastika flies like an evil omen above the ruins

160. Towards the end of January 1943 the senseless sacrifice of thousands of German soldiers came grimly to an end. The capitulation of the German troops took place on 31 January and 1 February 1943. Field Marshal Paulus *(left)* presents himself as a prisoner of war to the Soviet 64th Army. To the right are his adjutants, General Arthur Schmidt and Colonel Wilhelm Adam

161–163. Sober figures conceal untold suffering. According to ration strength, the German Sixth Army numbered 323,000 men. Of these, 290,000 were encircled at Stalingrad. After the wounded had been flown out, Field Marshal Paulus was left with 220,000 men. Of these, 91,000 were taken prisoner by the Russians; some 5,500 prisoners survived

161

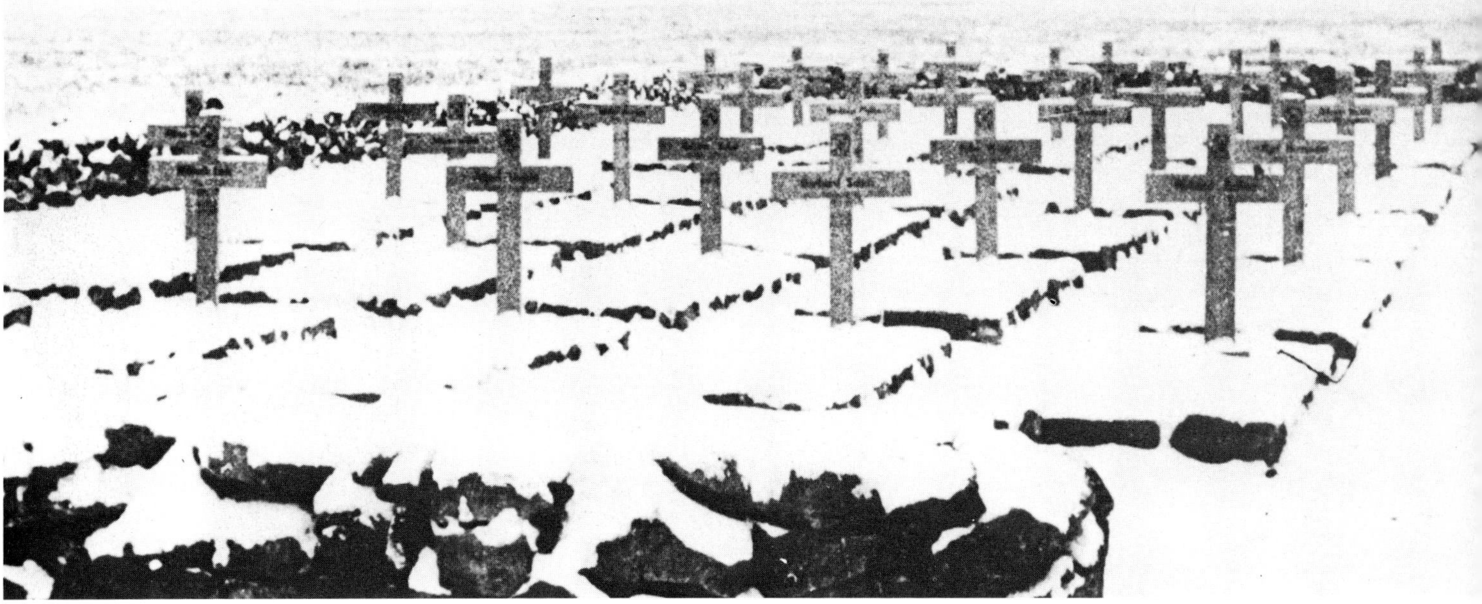

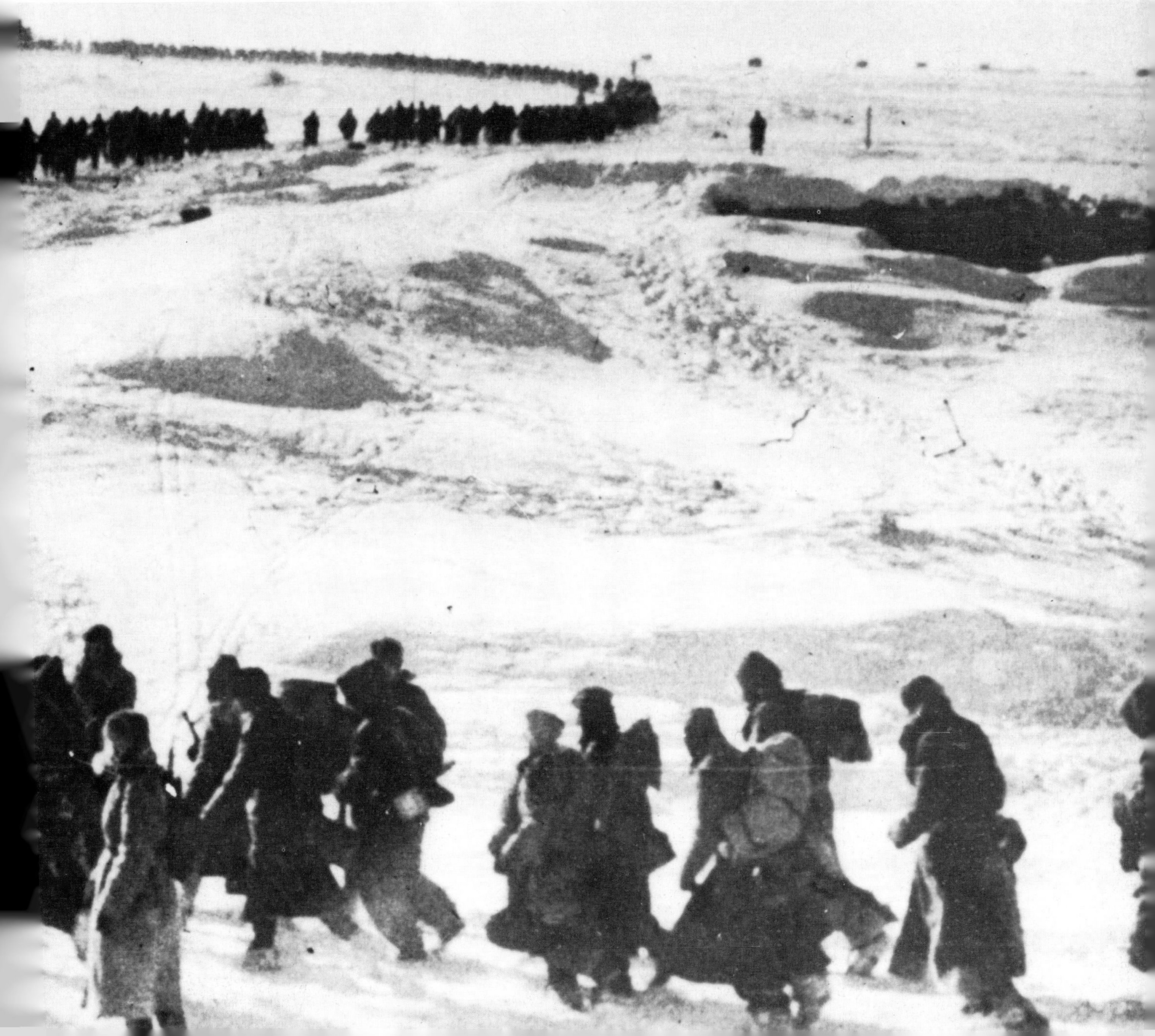

APPENDICES

Chronology of the German campaign against Russia from 22 June 1941 to 2 February 1943

Places mentioned in this book have been given the names in use at the time.

1941

22 June: German assault with three Army Groups launched at 03.15 hrs without declaration of war and along an 870-mile front. Air strikes on Soviet airfields. German drive on Brest-Litovsk. Germans capture Przemysl on the San. Rumania and Italy declare war on the Soviet Union.

23 June: Slovakia declares war on the Soviet Union.

24 June: German units take Kaunas and Vilna (Lithuania).

25 June: German panzer troops take Lutsk and Dubno (Ukraine). Collapse of Soviet counterattacks at Grodno and Rossieny (Lithuania).

26 June; Germans capture Daugavpils (Lithuania). German and Rumanian troops take Skulyany (Bessarabia). Finland declares war on the USSR.

27 June: Germans capture Riga. Germans encircle Soviet divisions at Minsk. Hungary declares war on the USSR.

28 June: Germans capture Liepaja (Libau), Brest-Litovsk and Kovel.

29 June: Germans encircle parts of Soviet West Front (General Pavlov) at Bialystok. German ski troops (Mountain Corps Norway) led by 'Dietl of Narvik' start drive on Murmansk.

30 June: Germans take Lvov. Stalin sets up Council of Defence.

1 July: Beginning of German-Finnish drive on Salla, which falls on 7 July.

2 July: Germans attack Moldavia. Marshal Timoshenko appointed Commander in Chief of Soviet West Front.

3 July: In his first broadcast since the German invasion, Stalin declares a 'Great Patriotic War' against German Fascism. Call for partisan warfare.

5 July: German Army Group South (von Rundstedt) begins to breach the Stalin Line.

6 July: German Sixth Army breaks through Stalin Line. Germans take Miropolye.

8 July: Hitler discloses his decision to raze Moscow and Leningrad to the ground 'lest we have to feed the population during the winter'.

9 July: Double battle of Bialystok and Minsk ends with collapse of Soviet West Front (Timoshenko). Approx. 324,000 Soviet prisoners. Germans take Zhitomir and Vitebsk. German Army Group North (von Leeb) takes Pskov and advances on Leningrad. General Halder, Chief of the German Army General Staff, considers that Germany has as good as won the war against the Soviet Union.

10 July: 'Karelian Army' launches offensive north of Lake Ladoga. Staff of Central Partisan Movement appointed in Moscow.

11 July: German panzers cross the Dnieper at Mogilev.

12 July: Anglo-Soviet Mutual Assistance Pact. Declaration that neither party will sign a separate peace with the Axis powers.

13 July: Soviet troops counterattack and capture Rogachev and Zhlobin in the Bobruysk sector. Germans capture Propoysk and Gorki.

14 July: Stalin calls for partisan warfare. Hitler orders German arms factories to switch to U-boats and aircraft, believing the issue in the East to be already decided in his favour.

16 July: Germans capture Smolensk. German and Rumanian troops take Kishinev. Hitler explains his objectives in the East to Göring, Bormann, Rosenberg and Keitel: break-up and maximum exploitation of all occupied areas of the USSR.

17 July: Germans set up Ministry for the Occupied Eastern Territories (Rosenberg) with Commissariats Ukraine (Koch) and 'Eastland' (Lohse).

18 July: German troops take Yelnya in the central sector and Velikiye-Luki. German and Rumanian troops cross the Dniester. Stalin calls on Churchill to form a Second Front in Europe.

19 July: Hitler orders Army Group Centre (von Bock) to continue the drive on Moscow but withdraws support units from Army Groups North (von Leeb) and South (von Rundstedt).

21 July: Soviet units recapture Velikiye-Luki.

21-22 July: First German air attack on Moscow.

23 July: Soviet counterattack in the Yelnya sector near Smolensk.

26 July: Germans wipe out Soviet troops in Mogilev sector.

31 July: Germans advance to Lake Ilmen. Beginning of Finnish offensive on Lake Ladoga.

3 August: Germans trap large Soviet force in Roslavl sector (38,000 prisoners). The Quartermaster General of the German High Command prepares the issue of winter clothing.

5 August: Army Group Centre (von Bock) liquidates Smolensk pocket (310,000 Soviet prisoners).

7 August: Stalin appoints himself Commander-in-Chief of the Red Army.

8 August: Liquidation of Uman pocket (103,000 Soviet prisoners).

12 August: Soviet counter-offensive near Staraya Russia south of Lake Ilmen.

14 August: Stalin makes agreement with Polish government in exile to set up an army of Polish prisoners of war under General Anders.

16 August: Germans capture Nikolayev dockyard on the Black Sea.

17 August: Germans capture Narva.

18 August: Germans establish bridgehead near Zaporozhye on the Dnieper. Fighting near Kairala (Kandalaksha Front, Finland).

20 August: Germans take Kherson on the Black Sea.

21 August: Hitler orders capture of Crimea and Donets Basin, encirclement of Soviet forces at Kiev and encirclement of Leningrad. Finnish forces drive on Vyborg.

25 August: Germans drive on Kiev from Gomel area. Germans capture Dniepropetrovsk.

26 August: Germans mop up Russian units in Velikiye-Luki sector. Memorandum from the German High Command, approved by Hitler, admits that

the Soviet campaign cannot now be finished before the end of 1941 and that all other operations (against British positions in the Middle East and North-West Africa) will have to be postponed until 1942.

7 September: German drive on Murmansk (Dietl) halted. German panzers break through at Konotop (Ukraine).

8 September: Germans cut all overland connections to Leningrad at Schlüsselburg. Germans capture Chernigov.

12 September: Start of German drive from Kremenchug bridgehead on the Dnieper.

14 September: Germans complete encirclement of the mass of the Soviet divisions (South-West Front) in the Kiev sector. Germans take Mirgorod.

18 September: Germans take Poltava (Ukraine).

19 September: Germans take Kiev.

21 September: Germans take Krasnograd.

24 September: Start of German drive on the Perekop isthmus, Crimea (von Manstein). Soviets drive back a Rumanian army near Melitopol.

25 September: Drive of German Army Group North (von Leeb) on Leningrad halted.

26 September: Germans liquidate Kiev pocket (665,000 Soviet prisoners).

29 September: German attack in the Crimea halted.

30 September: German panzer drive on Orel.

2 October: Start of German drive on Moscow (Operation Typhoon) by Army Group Centre (von Bock). Double battle of Vyazma and Bryansk. German Army Group South (von Rundstedt) advances on Kharkov and Kursk.

3 October: Germans take Orel.

5 October: Battle on the Sea of Azov.

6 October: Germans take Bryansk.

7 October: Germans take Vyazma, Berdyansk and Mariupol (Sea of Azov). Onset of winter. Hitler orders rejection of any capitulation by defenders of Moscow.

9 October: Hitler's Press Chief, Otto Dietrich, declares that the issue in the East has been decided and that the Soviet Union is beaten.

10 October: Germans liquidate Sea of Azov pocket (about 100,000 prisoners).

11 October: German panzers reach the Volga near Pogoreloye Gorodishche.

12 October: Germans occupy Kaluga on the Oka.

13 October: Germans occupy Kalinin, west of Moscow.

14 October: German drive on Murmansk called off. Germans take Rzhev in the Kalinin sector.

16 October: Rumanians occupy Odessa. Soviet government and the diplomatic corps leave Moscow for Kuybyshev on the Volga.

19 October: Stalin declares state of siege in Moscow.

20 October: German Army Group Centre wins Vyazma-Bryansk battle (673,000 prisoners).

21 October: Germans capture Stalino, west of the Donets Basin.

24 October: Germans occupy Kharkov and Belgorod (on the Donets).

27 October: German breakthrough at Perekop (Crimea). Germans take Kramatorsk.

1 November: Germans take Simferopol (Crimea).

3 November: Germans occupy Kursk.

4 November: Germans take Feodosiya (Crimea).

8 November: Germans cross the Volkhov and drive on Tikhvin.

15 November: Beginning of second phase of battle for Moscow.

19 November: Hitler declares that his troops will advance into the Caucasus Mountains and to the southern borders of the USSR in 1942.

21 November: Germans take Rostov-on-Don and Stalinogorsk near Moscow.

28 November: Germans reach the Volga-Moskva Canal. Germans retreat from Rostov.

5 December: Kalinin Front (Koniev) launches counter-offensive.

6 December: West Front (Zhukov) launches counter-offensive. Great Britain declares war on Finland, Rumania and Hungary.

7 December: Hitler passes 'Night and Fog' Decree: all persons 'endangering German security' are to vanish without trace into the 'night and fog' of Germany.

8 December: Hitler orders his divisions in the East to stand their ground.

9 December: Soviet troops restore railway link to Leningrad and occupy Tikhvin. The German divisions withdraw across the Rostov. China (Chiang Kai-shek) declares war on Germany.

10 December: Soviet troops break through at Livny.

11 December: Germany and Italy declare war on USA.

12 December: Bulgaria, Rumania and Hungary declare war on USA. Bulgaria declares war on Great Britain.

13 December: German troops withdraw in the Tula sector.

14 December: Germans evacuate Kalinin.

16 December: Hitler calls on his troops on the Eastern Front to put up 'fanatical resistance'.

17 December: German attack on Sebastopol (Crimea).

19 December: Field Marshal von Brauchitsch steps down. Hitler takes personal command of the German army.

20 December: German troops withdraw to their winter positions.

27 December: Soviet advance in the Kalinin sector.

29 December: Soviet troops breach lines of German Army Group Centre (von Bock). Germans evacuate Kerch (Crimea).

31 December: German attack on Sebastopol called off.

1942

2 January: Soviet breakthrough at Rzhev.

3 January: Germans encircled at Sukhinichi near Kaluga.

5 January: Soviet landing attempt at Yevpatoriya (Crimea) is beaten off. (Fighting continues until 8 January.)

8 January: Start of Soviet offensive on Lake Ilmen and in the Ostashkov sector.

11 January: Soviet breakthrough at Yukhnov.

15 January: German Army Group Centre (von Kluge) evacuates Kaluga salient and retires to winter positions.

18 January: Soviet breakthrough at Iziyum. Soviets encircle a German Army Corps in the Demyansk sector (Lake Ilmen). Germans recapture Feodosiya (Crimea). Kerch Peninsula cut off.

24 January: Germans relieve Sukhinichi near Kaluga.

1 February: Soviet advance on Vyazma.

3 February: German counterattack at Yukhnov (Vyazma sector) leads to encirclement of Soviet units.

13 March: Soviet attack on Kerch Peninsula.

15 March: On the occasion of 'German Heroes' Day', Hitler predicts the destruction of the Red Army in the summer of 1942.

20 March: Germans counterattack at Kerch.

5 April: Hitler gives instruction for German summer offensive (advance to the Volga, to the Caucasus and to the Iranian border).

15 April: Germans route Soviet troops encircled near Yukhnov (Vyazma sector) and take 6,000 prisoners.

28 April: Relief of German troops encircled near Demyansk.

8 May: Start of German offensive on Kerch front (von Manstein).

9 May: Start of Soviet drive on Kharkov from Donets bridgehead (Timoshenko).

17 May: Start of German counter-offensive against Marshal Timoshenko's units.

22 May: Germans encircle Soviet units advancing on Kharkov.

28 May: Battle of Kharkov ended. Germans take 239,000 Soviet prisoners.

7 June: Germans attack Sebastopol.

11 June: Agreement on principles of mutual aid between USSR and USA signed in Washington.

28 June: Start of German summer offensive from the Kursk sector.

30 June: German Sixth Army (Paulus) launches offensive in Belgorod sector.

1 July: Germans capture Sebastopol (von Manstein).

2 July: Start of German offensive in Sychevka salient.

4 July: German occupation of the Crimea concluded with the capture of the Khersonneskiy Peninsula (97,000 prisoners).

6 July: Germans capture Voronezh on the Don.

9 July: Start of German offensive in Kharkov sector.

12 July: Germans mop up Volkhov pocket (some 33,000 Soviet prisoners). Soviet forces destroyed in Sychevka sector (some 3,000 prisoners).

21 July: Germans cross the Don at Rostov.

23 July: Germans capture Rostov-on-Don.

26 July: German Army Group A (List) starts drive on Caucasus from the Don.

28 July: Directive by Soviet High Command at Stalingrad: 'Not one step backwards.'

30 July: Start of major operation to relieve Soviet West Front at Rzhev.

4 August: German troops cross the Aksay and start drive on Stalingrad.

6 August: German troops cross the Kuban near Armavir.

7 August: German Sixth Army (Paulus) attacks in Kalach sector.

9 August: Germans take Krasnodar and the port of Yeysk on the Sea of Azov.

11 august: German panzer advance in the Sukhinichi sector.

14 August: Germans cross the Kuban at Krasnodar.

19 August: Paulus orders Sixth Army to attack Stalingrad.

2 August: German advance in Sukhumi sector (Caucasus) brought to a halt.

23 August: Hitler orders attack on Leningrad (Operation 'Northern Light').

25 August: State of siege declared at Stalingrad.

27 August: Soviet advances on Schlüsselburg on the Leningrad front and also on the Volkhov front.

1 September: German and Rumanian troops cross the Kerch Straits and advance into the Taman Peninsula. Germans establish bridgehead on the Terek.

3 September: German units (von Seydlitz) advance on centre of Stalingrad.

6 September: Germans capture port of Novorossiysk on the Black Sea.

10 September: Soviet offensive on Leningrad front brought to a halt.

15 September: Start of Soviet drive on Voronezh.

24 September: Germans advance on the Black Sea port of Tuapse. General Halder, Chief of the German Army General Staff, is replaced by General Zeitzler.

6 October: Germans capture Malgobek in the Terek salient.

9 October: Army commissars abolished in USSR. Military commanders are given sole authority.

14 October: Hitler declares that German troops in the East are extremely well equipped for the winter of 1942/3; the Red Army has been greatly weakened by the recent engagements and is not as strong as it was in the spring; all German Army Groups must 'consider their present lines springboards for a German offensive in 1943 and hold them at all costs'.

18 October: German drive on Tuapse halted.

25 October: German offensive in the Caucasus. Soviet troops evacuate Nalchik.

1 November: Germans take Alagir in the Caucasus.

2 November: Germans take Ordzhonikidse in the Caucasus.

19 November: Major Soviet offensive on the Don smashes through Rumanian positions north of Stalingrad.

20 November: Start of Soviet offensive south of Stalingrad.

22 November: Soviet spearheads meet at Kalach and complete encirclement of German Sixth Army (Paulus). Hitler orders Sixth Army to adopt a hedgehog (all-round defensive) position and to await relief.

25 November: Eighth German Air Corps starts to airlift supplies to Stalingrad pocket. Daily average flown in is 95 tons instead of the promised 300 tons.

12 December: Strong German panzer concentrations (Hoth) advance from the Kotelnikovo sector to break through to the Sixth Army pocket at Stalingrad (Paulus).

16 December: Start of Soviet drive on Rostov. Soviet troops overrun Italian lines. Germans call off attack on Tuapse.

21 December: German panzer advance (Hoth) for the relief of Stalingrad halted on the Myshkova.

23 December: German attempts to relieve Stalingrad called off. Operation 'Thunderbolt' (massive breakout of Sixth Army) cannot be launched because Hitler refuses to sanction it.

24 December: Start of Soviet drive on Kotelnikovo. Russians smash the Rumanian defences.

28 December: German Army Group A (Caucasus) receives orders to retreat.

1943

1 January: German troops begin to retreat on Terek front. Germans evacuate Elista (Kalmuck SSR). Germans set up emergency units.

3 January: Hitler orders the capture or destruction of the Maykop oilfields, the securing of the Kerch Straits and the extension of the railway line to Kerch.

5 January: Hitler orders Field Marshal Milch to ensure Stalingrad airlift to the Sixth Army.

8 January: Soviet High Command sends surrender ultimatum to encircled German Sixth Army.

10 January: Soviet drive (Rokossovsky) to liquidate Stalingrad pocket.

12 January: Soviet troops on the Don smash through Hungarian and Italian lines. Germans in the Caucasus retreat to the Kuban bridgehead. Soviets attempt to restore overland link to Leningrad.

13 January: Germans retreat from Terek to the Nagutskoye-Alexsandrovskoye Line.

14 January: German Army General Staff proposes strengthening the Eastern Front by force. Lithuanians, Latvians and Estonians are to be conscripted for police or army duties.

15 January: Soviet troops capture Velikiye Luki.

17 January: A German panzer corps surrounded on the Don.

24 January: Advance of Soviet TransCaucasian Front halted at Novorossiysk-Krasnodar.

25 January: German Sixth Army (Paulus) at Stalingrad is split in two by Soviet advances into both northern and southern sectors. The last airstrip in Stalingrad is no longer serviceable. Germans retreat from Armavir and Voronezh.

26 January: Seven German divisions encircled in the Kastornoye sector.

31 January: Field Marshal Paulus capitulates in Stalingrad's southern pocket.

2 February: Capitulation of northern pocket brings the battle for Stalingrad to an end.

This chronology is based on:

Chronik des Zweiten Weltkrieges. Kalendarium militärischer und politischer Ereignisse 1939–1945, Hillgruber and Hümmelchen; Düsseldorf, 1978

Der Zweite Weltkrieg. Bilder, Daten, Dokumente, Munich, 1983

Maps

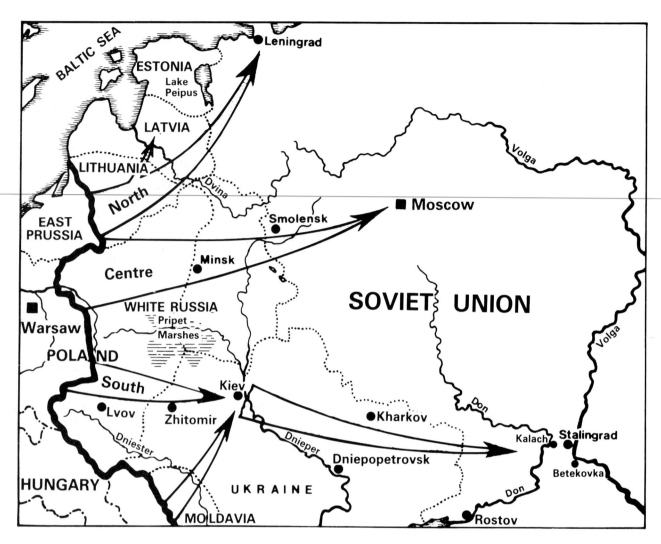

Above: Main thrust of the three German Army Groups during the so-called Eastern Campaign: Army Group North towards Leningrad; Army Group Centre towards Moscow; and Army Group South towards the Volga and Stalingrad.

Opposite above: (after a sketch by Field Marshal Paulus, amplified later with data supplied by Doerr): Position in the Stalingrad pocket on 10 January 1943. After countless Soviet incursions into the pocket, the encircled German units were squeezed into two small areas by 26 January. The southern island held out until 31 January, the northern until 2 February. The Germans then capitulated. On the map, the roman numbers refer to corps and the arabic numbers to army groups and divisions; 'U.Tle.d.rum.I.R.86' means 'And parts of 86 Romanian Infantry Regiment'.

Opposite below: Positions of German units left in the Stalingrad pocket. At the time the Pitomnik and Gumrak airfields were still in full use. The solid outer black line indicates the front line at the beginning of December 1943, the inner lines show the position on 13 January, and the two black splotches near Stalingrad are the tiny islands that remained on 26 January.

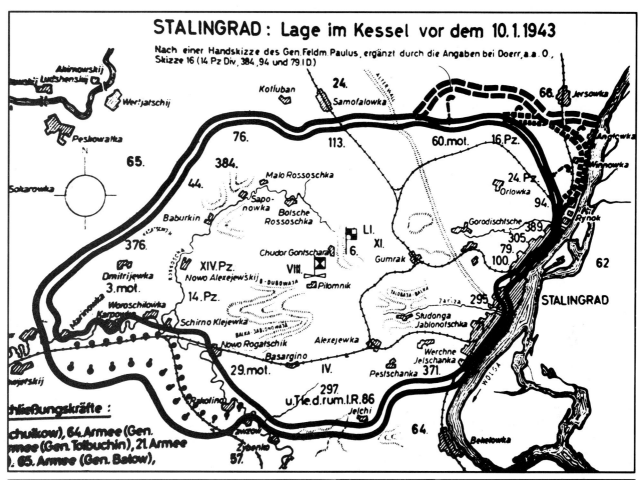

STALINGRAD: Lage im Kessel vor dem 10.1.1943

Nach einer Handskizze des Gen. Feldm. Paulus, ergänzt durch die Angaben bei Doerr, a.a.O.,
Skizze 16 (14.Pz.Div, 384,94 und 79.I.D.)

Der Stalingradkessel

FRONTVERLAUF
Anfang Dez. ▬▬▬
Am 13.1.43 ▭▭▭
Am 26.1.43 ᴧᴧᴧ

Maßstab etwa
1 : 400 000

Documents

Hitler's Order of 17 November 1942

Führer Decree of 17 November 1942 concerning capture of Stalingrad by Sixth Army

To Army High Comm. 6, Sect. Ia
AHQ 17 November 1942
13.15 hrs
SECRET
KR = Teleprint to Gen. Comm. LI Army Corps
Forw.: to Gen. Comm. VIII Air Corps

The following Führer Decree is to be communicated by word of mouth to all commanding officers engaged at Stalingrad down to and including Reg. Cdr:
'I am acquainted with the difficulties of the battle for Stalingrad and the diminishing operational strength. Ice drifting on the Volga, however, is now causing even greater difficulties for the Russians. If we exploit this breathing space we shall avoid a great deal of bloodshed later on. I accordingly expect that the High Command, with all its repeatedly proven energy, and the troops, with their frequently displayed courage, will again do everything in their power to break through to the Volga at least at the gun factory and at the steel works, and occupy these parts of the city.
Luftwaffe and Artillery must do all they can to prepare and support this attack.
The Führer
signed: Adolf Hitler

I am confident that this order will give our brave troops fresh impetus.
signed: Paulus
AHC 6 Ia No. 4640/42g.

General Paulus to Hitler on 23 November 1942

Paulus to Hitler, 23.11.42, concerning breakout of Sixth Army
Radio Mess. (draft) CO Sixth Army, to AHC. Forw: Army Gr B, 23.11.42, 21.30 hrs

Mein Führer!
Since receipt of your radio message of the evening of 22.11, the situation has been developing extremely rapidly. We have been unable to close the pocket in the south-west and the west. Enemy breaches here are imminent. Ammunition and fuel are running out. Numerous batteries and anti-tank guns have fired their last rounds. Adequate supplies cannot be provided in time.
The Army is facing annihilation at short notice unless the enemy, who is attacking from the south and the west, can be destroyed by the concentration of all our forces. To that end all divisions from Stalingrad should be withdrawn forthwith as well as the necessary larger forces from the northern front. The breakout will inevitably have to be in the south-west, since the eastern and northern fronts can no longer be held after so much depletion of our strength. We shall have to sacrifice large amounts of materials but shall be saving the majority of our valuable fighting men as well as at least part of the materials.
I take full responsibility for this grave message when I add that Generals Heitz, von Seydlitz, Strecker, Hube and Jaenecke have arrived at an identical assessment of the situation.
In view of this situation I once more request freedom of action.
Heil mein Führer!
signed: Paulus

Hitler's Order of 24 November 1942

Führer Decision of 24.11.42 re holding of Sixth Army position and relief. Radio Mess. to OKH GenStH/OpDiv/(I/SB) No. 420 960/42 of 24.11.42, 01.40 hrs, rec. CO A6 at 08.30 hrs

To the Sixth Army
Führer Decision:
The Führer intends to concentrate Sixth Army in the sector of the present Volga front, the present northern front of LI Army Corps, and then along the general line ref. pt 564 – Karpovka – Marinovka. To that end the north-west units of the Sixth Army will be withdrawn across the Don between Nizhniy Gerasimov and Malyy and then behind the general line ref. pt 564 Marinovka, so that the least possible amount of heavy armour and equipment is abandoned. Simultaneously the area of concentration will be extended by a drive to the south-west in the general direction of Kotelnikovo.

Concentration of mobile forces round Kotelnikovo (Second Panz. Div.) initiated with orders to prepare meeting in Businovka direction. Present Volga front and northern front of LI Army Corps to be held at all costs. Air drops about to be augmented by deployment of another 100 Ju.

Order by General Paulus of 24 November 1942

CO Sixth Army to Army Corps of 24.11.42, re continuation of fighting
Radio Mess. AHC 6/Ia of 24.11.42, 11.15 hrs

1. The Army will consolidate the sector: Stalingrad – former northern front – bridgehead on western bank of Don – Sokarevskiy – Illarionovskiy – Marinovka – present front of IV Army Corps, and will hold it until further notice.

Subsequent intention: Drive to south-west while holding northern front as long as possible.
2. To that end, LI Army Corps will hold its positions (Stalingrad – Spartakovka – elev. 139.7 – former northern front) until further notice. The Corps will prepare to take the line Chem. Factory – Gorodische – right wing 113th Inf. Div.

Heitz Group will hold its former northern front east of the Don and bridgehead west of Don. Contraction of front on western wing of 76th Inf. Div. should be attempted.

This group will conduct units of LI Corps and XIV Panzer Corps not deployed in the bridgehead across the Don and will place them under the command of CO XIV Panzer Corps.

XIV Panzer Corps will secure the western flank of the Army along the general line Sokarevskiy – Illarionovskiy – Marinovka (excl.) Enemy tanks reported in this sector should be destroyed. Sixth von Arnim's group and those sections of XIV Panzer Corps and XI Army Corps brought across the river by VIII Army Corps together with 3rd Inf. Div. (motorized) to be placed under command of XIV Panzer Corps.

IV Army Corps will hold its present position.
3. *It is most important* that all commanding officers should keep a firm grip on their men, remove with them the maximum amount of arms and equipment and, by taking the strictest disciplinary measures, lead their men, despite the harsh conditions and difficulties, to their assigned positions.

signed: Paulus
[Author's note: On 25 November 1942, General Schmidt altered this order following receipt of the Führer Decree of 24 November 1942. The phrase 'as long as possible' was deleted from 1., and the words 'a second line' were added to 2.]

Memorandum by General von Seydlitz of 25 November 1942

Art. Gen. v. Seydlitz-Kurzbach, OC LI AC to COC Sixth Army on 25.11.42 re Army Order of 24.11.42. Copy by AHC to COs Army Gr Don; COs LI AC No. 603/42 GCF 25.11.42, rec. Army Gr. Don 28.11.42.

In receipt of the Army Order of 24 November 1942 for the continuation of fighting, and fully cognizant of the gravity of the situation, I feel obliged to resubmit in writing my opinion which has been strengthened further by events during the past 24 hours.

The Army is faced with a clear *either-or*: *Breakthrough* to the south-west in the general direction of Kotelnikov or *annihilation* within a few days. This assessment is based on a sober evaluation of the actual situation.

1. Since practically no supplies were available at the beginning of the battle, the *supply position must be a crucial factor in any final decision*. State of supplies of LI AC on evening of 23.11 [not reproduced].

The figures speak for themselves.

Even the minor skirmishes of the past few days have led to an appreciable decrease in the supply of ammunition. If, as can be expected daily, the Corps is attacked along the entire front, its supply of ammunition will be completely exhausted within 1–3 days. It is unlikely that the supply position of the other Army Corps, which have been engaged in major battle for several days, is any better.

From the attached figures it follows that the adequate airlifting of supplies for LI Corps is doubtful and for the entire Army out of the question. What supplies 30 Ju can fly in (on 30.11) or the further 100 Ju that have been promised can be no more than a drop in the ocean. To base our hopes on them is grasping at a straw. It is not clear where the much larger number of Jus needed is to come from. If they are available at all, they would first have to be flown in from all over Europe and North Africa. Because of the distances involved, their own fuel requirements would be so great that, with the general fuel shortages we have experienced, the whole operation looks questionable, quite apart from the operational consequences of this measure for the war effort as a whole. Even if 500 instead of the promised 130 aircraft could be flown in each day, they could not carry more than 1,000 tons of material, which is inadequate for the needs of an army of 200,000 men engaged in major battle and that has run out of supplies. At best they can fly in the most essential fuel supplies, a small fraction of the requirement for various types of ammunition and perhaps also a fraction of the food rations as well. Within a few days, all the horses will have perished. Tactical manoeuvrability will have been restricted even further, the distribution of supplies to the troops rendered considerably more difficult, and the fuel requirement stepped up even further.

There is little doubt that the bulk of the weather-proof Russian fighter planes will be used to intercept the incoming transport planes and to attack the Pitomnik and Pestkovatka airfields, the only ones suited to major airlifts. Considerable losses are inevitable, and uninterrupted fighter support for the long approach and the two airfields can hardly be taken for granted. Weather conditions, too, are bound to affect the airlift.

Because of the impossibility of bringing in sufficient supplies by air, the exhaustion of the remaining supplies within a few days – about 3–5 days for ammunition – can at best be slightly delayed but not prevented. Making available provisions go further is to some extent in our own hands (LI Army Corps was ordered to stretch them by 100 per cent three days ago). But when it comes to stretching the fuel and ammuntion supplies, we are wholly dependent on the enemy.

2. *The probable actions of the enemy*, who can look forward to a battle of annihilation of classical proportions, is easy to predict. Familiarity with his previous tactics leads one to suppose that he will continue his attacks on the encircled Sixth Army with undiminished ferocity. We must also credit the enemy with being able to realize that he must destroy the Sixth Army before our relief measures can be put into effect. We know from past experience that sacrifice of human lives will not deter him. Our successful defence tactics, especially on 24.11, and his heavy losses must not lead us into self-deception.

Moreover, the enemy cannot be entirely unfamiliar with our supply problems. The more persistently and fiercely he attacks, the more quickly will we run out of ammunition. Even if every one of his attacks should be repulsed, he will nevertheless achieve final victory if we have exhausted our ammunition and become defenceless. To deny him this realization means counting on his mistakes. This has led to defeat throughout military history. It would in any case be an inordinate risk which, with the collapse of the Sixth

Army, would have the gravest consequences upon the duration of the war and perhaps also on its final outcome.

3. In purely operational terms, it follows that the Sixth Army can only escape destruction in the hedgehog position if relief proves so effective that, in a few, *i.e. approximately five days*, the enemy is forced to stop his attacks. *There are no indications whatsoever that this can be done.* If relief cannot arrive until later, then our state of defencelessness will be such that the destruction of the Sixth Army is inevitable.

It is impossible to foresee what measures the Army High Command can take to relieve the Sixth Army. Relief from the west *can* only be a long way off since the only covering forces are west of the Upper Chir at Oblivskaya on the Lower Chir, so that relief forces will have to be assembled far from the Sixth Army. Organizing a force strong enough to effect a *quick* breakthrough across the Don and covering its northern flank will take weeks as the Millerovo railway line is largely unserviceable. Add to this the time needed for the operation itself, which because of the bad weather and the short winter days is considerably longer than in the summer.

The deployment of two panzer divisions at Kotelnikovo for a relief operation from the south, and their arrival, will take at least ten days. The prospect of a *quick* breach of the enemy lines is gravely hampered by the need to cover the lengthening flanks, and particularly the eastern flank, of the relief force, not to mention the state of the divisions and the question of whether or not two panzer divisions are enough. The speeding up of the deployment of relief forces by throwing in a larger number of motorized columns cannot be considered a possibility – neither the columns nor the fuel can be available, or they would have been used for supplying the exposed Stalingrad front much earlier, when the distances involved were much smaller.

4. The prospect of relief within a period when the arrival of supplies is still likely to make a difference is therefore *as good as nil*. The order by the High Command to hold the hedgehog position until aid arrives is obviously based on false assumptions. It cannot be implemented and would inevitably lead to disaster for the Sixth Army. If the Army is to be saved, then *the order must be revoked at once, or else the Army must immediately act as if it had been.*

The idea of sacrificing the Army deliberately must, in view of the operational, political and moral consequences, be out of the question.

5. A comparison of the timescale of supply and operational measures with that of probable enemy actions leads to so obvious a conclusion that further arguments are redundant. Nevertheless I would draw attention to the following facts, all of which point in the same direction:
a) The far from stabilized position on the *south-western front* of the hedgehog.
b) The *northern front* cannot withstand a concentrated enemy attack for any great length of time, since, following the withdrawal of the 16th Panzer Div. and later of the 3rd Inf. Div. (mot.), the northern front had to be moved back to hold what is admittedly a shorter but also an almost completely undeveloped line.
c) The strained situation on the *southern front*.
d) The greatly depleted *Volga front* has lost much of its striking power, which will be particularly felt when, as is to be expected soon, the river is completely iced over and another obstacle in the enemy's way has thus been removed.
e) Lack of ammunition has impeded the continuous replacement of men deployed at the enemy Volga bridgehead, where earlier enemy attacks have been tying down all reserves.
f) The *condition* of the divisions which have been bled dry in the drive on Stalingrad.
g) The Army has been tightly massed into a *barren area of steppe* which offers little usable shelter or practicable cover so that men and material are completely exposed to the weather and enemy air attacks.
h) *Impending winter conditions* with an almost total lack of heating fuel along the greater part of the present lines.
i) Inadequate support by the *Luftwaffe* because of lack of suitable operational bases. There is *no anti-aircraft support* because all available anti-aircraft units have been diverted to anti-tank defence.

Any comparison of the present position with conditions in the Demyansk pocket last year can only lead to dangerous conclusions. There, the difficult terrain favoured the defence. The distance from the German front was very much less. An encircled Corps needs significantly fewer supplies than an Army; in particular far fewer heavy weapons (panzers, heavy guns, mortars) had to be supplied with ammunition than are indispensable here in the barren steppes. Despite the shorter distance to the German front the creation of a very narrow corridor to the Demyansk pocket took *weeks* of heavy winter battles.

6. The alternatives are clear:
Either the Sixth Army *continues to hold* its

defensive hedgehog position until it has run out of ammunition, i.e. has become totally helpless. Since, with the certain continuation and probable extension of enemy attacks against what are still relatively quiet sectors of the front, this state of affairs is due to occur well before effective relief can arrive, a passive response means the *end of the Army*.

Or, in an effective operation, the Army can break out of its encirclement.

That is only possible if the Army, by stripping the northern and Volga fronts of troops, i.e. by shortening the front, can release enough combat forces to launch an attack on the southern front, and, after surrendering Stalingrad, break through at the enemy's weakest point, i.e. in the Kotelnikovo direction. This decision would involve abandoning considerable quantities of material, but offers the prospect of smashing the southern jaw of the Soviet pincer, thus saving a major part of the Army and its equipment for further operations. As a result a section of the enemy force will continue to be tied down, whereas with the annihilation of the Army in the hedgehog position the enemy will have a completely free hand. To the outside, the operation can be presented in a way that will help to preserve morale: 'After the total destruction of Stalingrad, centre of the Soviet arms industry, the Sixth Army, having first liquidated an enemy concentration on the Volga, has been withdrawn.'

The chances of success of a breakout are the greater as previous engagements have shown that the enemy infantry does not stand very firm on open terrain, and as some of our forces are still holding their positions along short stretches east of the Don and in the Aksay sector. In view of the pressing tim factor, the breakout must be started and completed *without delay*. Any delay reduces its prospects. Any delay cuts down the number of fighting men and the ammuntion. With every delay the enemy in the breakout sector becomes stronger and can bring up more support against the Kotelnikovo group. Every delay reduces our fighting strength by the decimation of horses and the consequent immobilization of horsedrawn guns.

Unless the Army High Command revokes the order to hold the hedgehog position immediately, my own conscience and responsibility to the Army and the German people impose the *imperative duty* to seize the freedom of action curtailed by the previous order and to use what little time is left to avoid utter disaster by a breakout attempt. The complete destruction of 200,000 fighting men and their entire supply of material and equipment is at stake.

There is no other choice.

signed: von Seydlitz
Artillery General

[Note by Chief of German Army General Staff: We do not have to cudgel the Führer's brain and Gen. von Seydlitz does not have to cudgel that of the C-in-C.]

These documents are taken from:

Stalingrad. Analyse und Dokumentation einer Schlacht, Manfred Kehrig, Stuttgart, 3rd edition, 1979

Kriegstagebuch des Oberkommandos der Wehrmacht (War Diary of the OKH) *1940-1945*, ed. by von Schramm with the collaboration of Hillgruber, Hubatsch and Jacobsen, Von Greiner and Schramm: Coblenz and Munich, 1961-4

Colour Photography during
the Second World War

Nowadays people seem to take it for granted that any publication on the Second World War should contain colour photographs. However, research for this book has shown that while official handouts are not hard to find, amateur photographers had a very difficult time capturing contemporary events in pictures, and particularly in colour.

During the Second World War, film was rationed in Germany, and even at the beginning of the war amateurs without connections had very limited access to filming material. As one of the photographers whose work is included in this book put it, only those who seemed to warrant it for propaganda purposes could obtain any. However, photographic establishments in the larger cities of German-occupied Poland were able to procure films more readily and over a longer period than those inside the Reich. It was from these that the photographers in this book acquired the bulk of their photographic material. One of them, moreover, had sufficient foresight to lay in a stock of films in 1938, for the express purpose of keeping a private record should war break out. Anticipating the coming shortages, he acquired 300 films, for what, at the time, was a very considerable outlay.

In 1936, Agfa brought out the first amateur colour reversal film (12° DIN), but once war was declared, counter sales were severely restricted.

At the time, it was unusual to use colour photography for propaganda purposes. Heroic themes, for instance in Nazi magazines, were generally illustrated by graphic artists.

The photographs reproduced in this book were taken with Leica and Kodak cameras which have survived the war and can still be used today.

German front-line reports were compiled by members of Propaganda Companies known as PK-reporters for short. The German Ministry of National Education and Propaganda and the *Wehrmacht* High Command jointly laid down the duties of all PKs. By August 1938, four Propaganda Companies had been set up, and at the outbreak of war the *Wehrmacht* could call on the services of thirteen.

These companies were not attached to any particular units and included writers, photographers and cameramen. The pictures taken were sent back to the Picture Press Bureau.

When Germany invaded the Soviet Union, it was found that a greater number of PK-reporters were needed than could be called upon. Even before the beginning of the campaign – in the spring of 1941 and again in the summer of 1941 – the Army High Command had set up special PK-reporter training courses. Nearly all the men detailed to these courses had done their basic military training. Approximately 300 film reporters completed technical courses at the State Film Institute and the Hansa School in Berlin. Their teachers were PK veterans and civilians from the photographic and film industry.

Even so, there was a shortage of professional cameramen and photographers for deployment at the front; many had already been killed. In these circumstances, the authorities decided to recruit members of the German League of Miniature and Amateur Photographers, and special photographic training then usually went hand in hand with military training. The following types of cine camera were the most popular: Ariflex hand-held camera, Askania Z and Siemens-D 16 mm cine cameras. The most common still cameras were Rolleis and Leicas. Goebbels had expressly ordered his PK-reporters to use German equipment.

This book includes a few photographs taken by a former PK-reporter and intended for his private use, but the great majority of the photographs have come from two amateurs who also served as soldiers at the front. It is this which gives these photographs their special authenticity.

It was extremely unusual, because it was forbidden, for soldiers outside the Propaganda Companies to take cameras and film into the field. The two amateurs were both clergymen, one serving in the ranks and the other as a chaplain. The third had been a professional photographer before being called up. After special training in Berlin he was attached to the Sixth Army with his PK unit in 1942, with orders to film the war for the official newsreel.

Whereas the first two photographers made notes and kept diaries, the third wrote letters to his wife – more than 300 all told until his death at Stalingrad. In these letters he repeatedly asked his wife not to open the colour films sent to her by the Agfa development section, but to leave them in their original cardboard tubes where they would suffer least damage.

The chaplain was able to arrange for fellow soldiers to supply him with films from base. The professional photographer was able to order some of his films from his former employer, who put them to one side for him.

The ordinary soldier was not allowed to carry bulky private possessions beyond the barest minimum. In particular, the use of binoculars and cameras had to be approved by his superiors. It was only because one of the photographers served in a PK unit and declared that his private photographers were part of his 'professional' work that he was allowed to use his camera freely. The chaplain was a special case, and as such was simply left alone with his camera. The other clergyman, who served in the ranks, was given permission to take photographs by a superior who knew that he was a pastor in civilian life. He was even given official instructions to make a pictorial record of his unit's progress against the day of final victory.

It borders on the miraculous that these colour photographs should have been preserved for more than forty years. It was difficult enough to bring them back from the front line. The films then had to lie about for weeks in a kitbag, inside some vehicle or in a tent before the photographer could reach an army post office and send them home to be developed. During that time the films and cameras may have had to withstand temperatures as high as 40°C and as low as minus 40°C. Not surprisingly, the photographs printed in this book have streaks and scratches, bearing witness to the effect of snow, rain and sandstorms. They reached the development tank along the most adventurous routes, and even then had to survive the ravages of the war in Germany.

These colour photographs from the front lines have meanwhile achieved the status of documents – records of the everyday reality of war from the viewpoint of the common soldier. To preserve them as a reminder and a warning is one of the aims of this book.

Herbert Kraft